W9-BCU-107

WITHDRAWN
FROM
COLLECTION

FORDHAM
UNIVERSITY
LIBRARIES

THE
END OF THE
MODERN
AGE

THE
END OF THE
MODERN
AGE

Allen Wheelis

Basic Books, Inc., Publishers

NEW YORK   LONDON

BD
450
· W 75
cop 3

Fordham University
LIBRARY
AT
LINCOLN CENTER
New York N.Y.

© 1971 by Basic Books, Inc.
Library of Congress Catalog Number 77–173833
SBN 465-01971–4
Manufactured in the United States of America
DESIGNED BY THE INKWELL STUDIO

for Joan

But as for certain truth, no man has known it,
Nor will he know it; neither of the gods,
Nor yet of the things of which I speak.
And even if he were by chance to utter
The final truth, he would himself not know it;
For all is but a woven web of guesses.

XENOPHANES

Contents

I

THE VISION
OF
THE MODERN
AGE

THE AGE is ending, the house is coming down—all the rafters, all the towers, all the clocks. It was built of a dream. The dream closes.

The character of an age derives from its vision of man's relation to the world. During the Middle Ages this vision portrayed man as child to heavenly father, sojourner in this land, on trial under watchful eyes, using this life to prepare for the next, seeing death as a door to the City of God. The remote arms of our Father was the ultimate goal.

The vision which has determined the Modern Age is this: *Man can know the world by the unaided effort of reason.*

No longer need man be intimidated by its danger, its complexity, its grandeur, its mystery. No longer need he get down on his knees to ask God to reveal it to him. He will seize it in the grip of intellect, pick it up, turn it over, take it apart. He will be subject, the world will be object; he will be an inquiring spirit, the world will be a thing. And however aggressively spirit probes into things, the nature of things will not be altered, nor will spirit be affected by the processes of knowing: for the world of spirit and the world of things do not touch.

Knowing the world will not, however, be disinterested and esthetic, as when one takes an apple in his hand, feels the smoothness and roundness, admires the red color, enjoys the sweetness; it will be interested and tendentious, it will serve power. For man, at the beginning of the Modern Age, is no longer a primitive, appalled by thunder and lightning; he is devious and sophisticated, has surmised that nature has secrets, that the variety, the unending panorama, derive from nature's laws, that he who knows these laws will control nature's forces. "I perceived it to be possible," wrote Descartes, "to arrive at knowledge highly useful in life, and instead of the speculative philosophy usually taught in the schools, to discover a practical [method] by means of which, knowing the force and action of fire, water, air, the stars, the heavens, and all the other bodies that surround us, as distinctly as we know the various crafts of our artisans, we might also apply them in the same way to all the uses to which they are adapted, and thus render ourselves the lords and possessors of nature." [1]

The existence of man could have been asserted as truly on the basis of love as upon thought, with no loss of logic and perhaps some gain in goodness, but

Descartes recognized himself most profoundly in the ability to think, and all of us who followed have chosen likewise. We have built our identity upon the analytic and reductive function. We believe the mind of man a match for the universe, that reason can assail any stronghold of mystery, that knowledge is power. From this cognitive vision comes the special quality of the Modern Age.

24 May, 1543. In the town of Frauenburg in East Prussia, in the northwest tower of the fortified wall, an old man lies dying, in his hands the first copy of his book *On the Revolutions of the Heavenly Spheres*. The medieval world is hundreds of years old, God's in his heaven. In the street lepers shake their rattles, bells are ringing, a procession passes, players and musicians. Could we, standing there, hearing the iron ring of cart wheel on cobblestone, have known that the old man fingering his Latin text, humbly dedicated to Pope Paul III, is a destroyer of the old world, a founding father of the one to come?

22 June, 1633. In the church of Santa Maria sopra Minerva in Rome Galileo recants his support of the condemned doctrine of Copernicus. The scientist is on his knees, head bowed. Before him sit ten cardinals in scarlet splendor, empowered to torture, empowered to kill, empowered to save. When they bid him rise, he rises, says nothing. Plague is in the streets, the bells toll. Could we even then know the

age is ending? Almost a hundred years have passed. Luther has split the Church, Kepler has reduced the divine circle of planets to flawed ellipse, and still we might not know.

We think of history as a freight train of events approaching the Modern Age; we look down the rails into the past and the black speck seems motionless. We are bemused: it is the fast express, hurtles toward us at breakneck speed, and our age is no metropolis, but a whistle stop on the plains, and it flashes by us without pause into the darkness of future. We are blinded by dust confused by thunder, tumult; and the bright vision is lost, as if on first acquaintance, before we could fix its face in heart and memory. There had seemed to be so much time; now it's gone.

The vision of the Modern Age is a Promethean leap in pride. While it does not usurp God's role, does not yet claim omnipotence for man, it makes a point of recognizing no limits. It alleges that the universe moves by forces which are blind, that man, therefore, possesses mind at the summit. No intelligence, no planning, no consciousness operates above him, and nothing, therefore, can set a priori limits to what he may think, accomplish, understand. The universe is vast, mysterious, hazardous, but as it is a machine, functions by law, man may aspire to know it and hence control it. For centuries man had toiled humbly in God's vineyard; now he owns it, is tinkering curiously with the wine press.

Some of the greatest achievements of science—those of Copernicus, of Darwin, and of Freud—are said to have been blows to man's ego, locating him less centrally in the universe, less uniquely in the order of living things, with dirtier hands. We are thereby reduced in significance, it is said, are humiliated, and would oppose this vision, reject these findings, but are forced to accept because the reduction has been arrived at by the objective methods of science. "The sanctity of all protoplasm," writes Harlow Shapley,

has practically disappeared in this, the heroic age of the physical sciences, when knowledge of the material universe, its content, structure, and dimensions, has so completely overthrown egocentrism. It should sufficiently deflate the organism, you would think, to find that his fountain of energy, the sun, is a dwarf star among thousands of millions of stars; to find that this star around which his little parasitic earth will-lessly plods is so far from the center of the known stellar universe that sunlight, with its incomprehensively high velocity, cannot reach that center in a thousand generations of vain men.[2]

In such sentiments we are devious: while pretending fortitude about loss of status, we covertly pat ourselves on the back for allegiance to truth. There's been no loss of status. These discoveries, in addition to being in themselves great instances of man's ability to know the world, and hence better to control it, are seen as proof of the validity of objective method, of the scope of man's vision. Man as subject can take even himself as object, can accept what comes therefrom, however it detract from his sense of being special. Man here becomes greater than gods, for gods are vain and could not accept diminishment. But man can. Behold! he does, and that's special indeed. There is concealed in this apparent modesty an arrogance of rare proportion.

What the new science destroyed was not pride of man but credibility of Christian story. "The privileged position of the earth," writes J. S. Bury,

had been a capital feature of the whole doctrine . . . taught by the church, and it had made that doctrine more specious than it might otherwise have seemed. Though the churches could reform their teaching to meet the new situation, the fact remained that the Christian Scheme sounded less plausible when the central importance of the human race was shown to be an illusion.[3]

There is a parallel between the character of an age and of a man. The character of a man derives from his actions, from those things he does so typically and repeatedly that they become established modes of behavior, having independent authority, in some sense operative even when quiescent—as stealing is active in the character of a thief even when he is not engaged in theft, as kindness is active in the character of a good man even when he is not helping a neighbor. We are what we do. But what we do derives in turn from an image of self, a vision antecedent to action. A child whose parents despise him learns what he is from the way they regard him, and the image so formed is likely to be that of an unworthy person who will be led by that image to anticipate not love but rejection. From such a self-image —which may be unconscious and hence inaccessible to reflection or to instruction—proceed aggressive and retaliatory actions which, becoming in time established modes of behavior, define the character of the man whom the child has become.

The character of an age bears analogy to this individual process. The quality of the Modern Age derives from what we have been doing during the last four hundred years, and so may be fairly characterized as the age of science and technology. But these scientific and technological things we have been doing derive from our collective self-image. The will that drives man on to great achievement depends on vision. The dream must come first to guide the effort, shape the leap, sustain the courage. In the sixteenth century man created an image of the limitless power of intelligence and found himself, dreamlike, saying, "Without help from God I can know the world"; and by virtue of believing it proceeded, in large measure, to make it true. The vast gain in reliable knowledge, in control of natural forces, is the result, and could not have come about had man continued to see himself as a humble worker in God's vineyard. By virtue of dreaming himself in charge, master of all that he can survey and understand—not boss of the operation exactly, but no one over him— he has made spectacular gains in knowing and now is drunk on wine. Pride goeth before a fall, and man is reeling and fall may be imminent, but we must grant pride its due: it made possible a great achievement in knowing. Such insight does not issue from modesty.

The medieval world is closed. There is no infinity of space: the stars are imbedded in a solid sphere which rotates daily around a static world; beyond the ninth sphere lies heaven. There is no infinity in time: the world is four thousand years old and will end within the foreseeable future. There is no infinity of learning: the final truth on every subject has already been written—by Aristotle for the natural world, by Plato for philosophy, by Euclid for mathematics, by Holy Writ for religion and cosmology. Within such a closed and finite universe, reason is not a revolutionary ferment, but rather interior decoration to an intellectual structure already finished.

Achievements of reason are offered to authority in humble manner, are forever wiping their feet and apologizing for themselves. Copernicus, who became in time a destroyer of this world, was in his own person a model citizen of the medieval world. "It is fitting for us," he wrote,

to follow the methods of the ancients strictly and to hold fast to their observations which have been handed down to us like a Testament. And to him who thinks that they are not to be entirely trusted in this respect, the gates of our Science are certainly closed. He will lie before that gate and spin the dreams of the deranged . . . and he will get what he deserves for believing that he can lend support to his own hallucinations by slandering the ancients.[4]

"Our ancestors," he writes in another context, "assumed a large number of celestial spheres for a special reason: to explain the apparent motion of the planets by the principle of regularity. For they thought it altogether absurd that a heavenly body should not always move with uniform velocity in a perfect circle." In Ptolemy's universe, however, the planets, although moving in perfect circles, did not in fact move at a uniform speed. "Having become aware of these defects," Copernicus wrote, "I often considered whether there could perhaps be found a more reasonable arrangement of circles . . . in which everything would move uniformly about its proper center, as the rule of absolute motion requires." [5]

"Thus Copernicus' first impulse to reform the Ptolemaic system," writes Arthur Koestler, "originated in his urge to remove a minor blemish from it, a feature which did not strictly conform to conservative Aristotelian principles. He was led to reversing the Ptolemaic system by his desire to preserve it— like the maniac who, pained by a mole on his beloved's cheek, cut off her head to restore her to perfection." [6]

Kepler, however, belonged to the world he was

creating. In his introduction to the *New Astronomy* he writes:

Now as regards the opinions of the saints about these matters of nature, I answer in one word, that in theology the weight is Authority, but in philosophy the weight of Reason alone is valid. Therefore a saint was Lanctantius, who denied the earth's rotundity; a saint was Augustine who admitted the rotundity, but denied that antipodes exist. Sacred is the Holy Office of our day, which admits the smallness of the earth but denies its motion: but to me more sacred than all these is Truth, when I, with all respect for the doctors of the Church, demonstrate from philosophy that the earth is round, circumhabited by antipodes, of a most insignificant smallness, and a swift wanderer among the stars.[7]

The issue, writes E. A. Burtt, was whether it is legitimate to take any other point of reference in astronomy than the earth: "The question went pretty deep, it meant not only, is the astronomical realm fundamentally geometrical, which almost anyone would grant, *but is the universe as a whole, including our earth, fundamentally mathematical in structure?*" [8]

Medieval times are called the Age of Faith, the modern period is called the Age of Reason. The distinction, as Carl Becker has pointed out, is inadequate: there is plenty of faith in our times—in science, in progress, in democracy—and there was plenty of reason in times before ours. The deliberate and conscious attempt to understand the universe was clearly established in the sixth century B.C. Scholasticism was pre-eminently an exercise of reason, and the edifice of thought left by Thomas Aquinas is a monument of rare scope and complexity. Reason is as old as man, and all of civilization may be viewed as its meandering growth.

The line between medieval and modern concerns the auspices under which reason is undertaken. In the Middle Ages reason is in the shadow of God, subject to curtailment and veto; God, acting through his deputies on earth, is the final authority. Reason is free to create and to discover only so long as it conforms to Holy Writ, and the main task always is to prepare for the life to come. Problem-solving activities concerning this world may be undertaken only with God's permission, may range only in permitted areas; discovered truth is subject to revealed truth; natural processes are not always natural, but liable to divine suspension. History is a series of ordained events issuing from inscrutable causes. However brilliant the investigator, therefore, he must work with humble heart, for he investigates at all only by God's leave. God determines the way things are, and God's will is inscrutable—beneficent but not to be known or measured.

The special quality of the Modern Age derives from the declaration that reason is independent, that there is no higher authority, that man's ability to understand is the pinnacle of whatever understanding is possible. There were important differences between the empiricism of Bacon, Locke, Berkeley, Hume, and Mill and the rationalism of Descartes, Spinoza, and Leibnitz; but they were united, writes Karl Popper, in the belief

that there was no need for any man to appeal to authority in matters of truth because each man carried the sources of knowledge in himself; either in his power of sense perception which he may use for the careful observation of nature, or in his power of intellectual intuition which he may use to distinguish truth from falsehood by refusing to accept any idea which is not clearly and distinctly perceived by the intellect.[9]

They are all, therefore, spokesmen for the Modern Age.

The mind of man, unaided, can know the world. This idea, the bell which woke the world from castled sleep, carried in its overtones those other ideas which define the Modern Age.

The intrinsic value of life on earth. For many centuries life had been viewed as a preparation, undeserving of serious attention, ". . . cramped by the belief," writes Charles Beard, "that man was a sinful creature born to trouble as the sparks fly upward, that the world would come to a close sometime, and that life on earth was not an end in itself but a kind of prelude to heaven or hell." [10] "All terrestrial beauty," writes Huizinga, "bore the stain of sin," [11] all striving was vanity. As the Medieval Age closed, man began to concern himself with this life as an end in itself. "It became possible," writes Beard, "to think of an immense future for mortal mankind, of the conquest of the material world in human interest, of providing the conditions for a good life on this planet without reference to any possible hereafter." [12]

The idea of progress. The classical ages had conceived of life as the endless repetition of a cycle, and found themselves, always, far from the Golden Age, of which they carried a vague racial memory, well into the phase of deterioration. "The rational soul," wrote Marcus Aurelius,

wanders around the whole world and through the encompassing void, and gazes into infinite time, and considers the periodic destructions and rebirths of the universe, and reflects that our posterity will see nothing new, and that our ancestors saw nothing greater than we have seen. A man of forty years, possessing the most moderate intelligence, may be said to have seen all that is past and all that is to come; so uniform is the world. [13]

Medieval man saw himself living in the final age, the one which would be terminated—"surprised like a sleeping household by a thief in the night" [14]—by the Day of Judgment. Until that time no improvement in the human lot was to be expected. With the Modern Age, for the first time, there opened before man the vision of an endless stretch of time during which he would progressively master the exigencies of this life, improve its quality, extend its benefits and blessings, and pursue happiness without guilt. Such progress, moreover, could be expected to occur quickly. "The particular phenomena of the arts and sciences are in reality but a handful," Bacon said; "the invention of all causes and sciences . . . the labor of but a few years." [15]

Optimism. In the late Middle Ages, writes Huizinga a "sombre melancholy weighs on people's souls. Whether we read a chronicle, a poem, a sermon, a legal document even, the same impression of immense sadness is produced by them all." [16] With the coming of the Modern Age, as no problem is beyond the reach of man, no problem is beyond solution. With this vision comes courage and hope. "Human powers," wrote Priestley in 1771,

will . . . be enlarged; nature, including both its materials, and its laws, will be more at our command; men will make their situation in this world abundantly more easy and comfortable; they will probably prolong their existence in it, and will daily grow more happy, each in himself, and more able (and, I believe, more disposed) to communicate happiness to others. Thus, whatever the beginning of this world, the end will be glorious and paradisiacal, beyond what imaginations can now conceive. [17]

Mechanism. In the Middle Ages man was child to a heavenly Father whose benevolent, if inscrutable, mind ruled the world. In the Modern Age the world becomes an independent and self-sufficient mechanism, exceptionlessly determined by universal laws which operate inexorably and exactly, which can never be suspended, and which in time may be fathomed by the inquiring spirit of man. "The great forces of nature, such as gravitation," writes Whitehead, "were entirely determined by the configurations of the masses. Thus the configurations determined their own changes, so that the circle of scientific thought was completely closed." [18] This universe is no longer provident and benevolent, but indifferent. "The ultimate source of things," wrote Hume, "has no more regard to good above ill than to heat above cold." [19]

The belief that man, by his own reason, can know the world had an immediate effect upon methods of observation. Facts become more important, are treated with more respect. Reason is no longer engaged in formal exercises about nature for the greater glory of God but in understanding the world in terms of natural causes; accuracy of observation and of measurement become crucial. Had Kepler felt free to ignore a discrepancy of eight minutes of arc between the predicted and observed position of Mars, he could have retained the dogma of circular motion. It was the taking seriously of that discrepancy that led to the discovery of the elliptical orbit. "What turned Kepler into the first law-maker of nature," writes Koestler,

was . . . *his introduction of physical causality into the formal geometry of the skies. . . .* So long as cosmology

was guided by purely geometrical rules of the game, re-
gardless of physical causes, discrepancies between
theory and fact could be overcome by inserting another
wheel into the system. In a universe moved by real,
physical forces, this was no longer possible. The revolution which freed thought from the stranglehold of ancient dogma, immediately created its own, rigorous dis-
cipline.[20]

Modern man would not only reach for truth on
his own authority, the truth he would grasp would
be different in quality. Throughout the Middle Ages
the truth achieved by man had been tentative, each
assertion accompanied by an anxious glance upward: "With your permission . . . by your gracious
leave . . . I beg to suggest . . ." To avoid the sin of
knowledge, knowing was made self-effacing, apolo-
getic, limited in scope and purpose. A jealous God
must ever be assured that man did not seriously un-
dertake to know the universe. Revelation was the
only source of certain knowledge.

Holy Writ records that God, in a fit of military ex-
pediency, commanded the sun to stand still in order
that Joshua might complete the massacre of the
Amorites in full daylight, thereby revealing that ordinarily the sun moves; and in 1616 the Church finally condemned the doctrine of Copernicus and forbade its teaching. It was Galileo's violation of this
injunction which brought him before the Inquisition.
The case turned, however, on an implicit issue of
deeper implication.

It is not known whether Copernicus on his death-
bed chanced to see the preface that, without his

knowledge, had been introduced into his book. It was written by Andreas Osiander, who anticipated that readers would take offense because the book declared the earth to move. "But if they are willing to examine the matter closely," Osiander wrote,

they will find that the author of this work has done nothing blameworthy. For it is the duty of an astronomer to compose the history of the celestial motions through careful and skillful observation. Then turning to the causes of these motions or hypotheses about them, he must conceive and devise, since he cannot in any way attain to the true causes, such hypotheses as, being assumed, enable the motions to be calculated directly from the principles of geometry, for the future as well as the past. The present author has performed both these duties excellently. For there is no need for these hypotheses to be true, or even to be at all like the truth; rather, one thing is sufficient for them—that they should yield calculations which agree with the observations . . . for if any causes are devised by the imagination, as indeed very many are, they are not put forward to convince anyone that they are true, but merely to provide a correct basis for calculation. Now when from time to time there are offered for one and the same motion different hypotheses . . . the astronomer will accept above all others the one which is the easiest to grasp. The philosopher will perhaps rather seek the semblance of truth. But neither of them will understand or state anything certain unless it has been divinely revealed to him. Let us therefore permit these new hypotheses to become known together with the ancient hypotheses, which are no more probable; let us do so especially because the new hypotheses are admirable and also simple, and bring with them a huge treasure of very skillful observation. So far as hypotheses are concerned, let no one expect anything certain from astronomy, which cannot furnish it, lest he accept as the truth ideas conceived for another purpose, and depart from this study a greater fool than when he entered it. Farewell.[21]

This Lutheran Osiander spoke here with the authentic voice of Rome: the theory was acceptable to the Church for whatever practical uses it might serve so long as it was not put forward as truth. Pope Gregory XIII had already sanctioned its use to good advantage in reform of the calendar.

Seventy-two years later Galileo is forcing the issue, and Cardinal Bellarmine, foremost theologian of the Church, is reiterating the same permissiveness and restating the same limit. ". . . Galileo will act prudently," he wrote,

. . . if he will speak hypothetically, *ex suppositione* . . . : to say that we give a better account of the appearances by supposing the earth to be moving, and the sun at rest, than we could if we used eccentrics and epicycles is to speak properly; there is no danger in that, and it is all that the mathematician requires. But to want to affirm that the sun, in very truth, is at the center of the universe and only rotates on its own axis without traveling from East to West, and that the earth is situated in the third sphere and revolves very swiftly around the sun, is a very dangerous attitude and one calculated not only to arouse all scholastic philosophers and theologians but also to injure our holy faith by contradicting the Scriptures. . . .[22]

Galileo was not at ease with this limitation. He believed that the theory, in addition to being useful, was also true; and this view, should it prevail, would imply that man alone, with but his own resources of reason, can know the world, discover its secrets. This was the threat to authority which the Church could not accept.

Galileo turned into the gale. "Methinks that in the discussion of natural problems," he wrote,

we ought not to begin at the authority of places of Scripture, but at sensible experiments and necessary illustration. . . . Nature, being inexorable and immutable, and never passing the bounds of the laws assigned her . . . I conceive that, concerning natural effects, that which either sensible experience sets before our eyes, or necessary demonstrations do prove unto us, ought not, on any account, to be called into question, much less condemned upon the testimony of texts of Scripture, which may, under their words, couch senses seemingly contrary thereto.[23]

He proceeds, then, to delimit the realm of science from the realm of faith.

Let us grant . . . that theology is conversant with the loftiest divine contemplation, and occupies the regal throne among the sciences by this dignity. But acquiring the highest authority in this way, if she does not descend to the lower and humbler speculations of the subordinate sciences and has no regard for them because they are not concerned with blessedness, then her professors should not arrogate to themselves the authority to decide on controversies in professions which they have neither studied nor practiced.[24]

The issue, therefore, is not freedom of thought, but truth. Copernicus had held his manuscript unpublished for more than thirty years, but it was not persecution he feared but ridicule. He had placed the sun in the center of the universe, but still needed forty-eight fictional epicycles to constrain the planets to circular orbits around it. The Church did not threaten him: in 1532 the personal secretary of Pope Leo X expounded the Copernican system to a receptive and well-disposed audience at the Vatican. Three years later Cardinal Schoenberg, writing from Rome, urged Copernicus to publish his work: "Therefore, learned man, without wishing to be inopportune, I beg you most emphatically to communicate your discovery to the learned world. . . ." [25]

Galileo was the intimate friend of Cardinals and of Popes, was free to experiment, to teach, and to publish. But this was not enough: he claimed for science the right to establish truth. Nature functions by law; the laws were "out there" waiting to be found, to be known. More and more they could be approximated by measurement, grasped by mathematical intuition, and finally, extrapolating beyond the diminishing margin of experimental error, demonstrated as absolute truth. Church and science, therefore, were contending for the same prize, the authority to establish truth, and both were claiming the right of final judgment. By ridiculing the position of the

Church Galileo provoked a confrontation. In this particular contest the Church won: Galileo was silenced about the motion of the earth. But the victory was Pyrrhic: thereafter with increasing frequency scientists claimed Galileo's position without having to accept his punishment.

"The new outlook did not take possession of society by any sudden breakthrough," writes Lewis Mumford;

. . . Rather the new ideology seeped into the common mind through a thousand cracks and fissures, against which no peremptory ecclesiastical edicts, aimed at a single book or a special doctrine, could in the long run have any effect. Actually, despite conflicts and skirmishes with the Church, science produced no martyrs. Whatever the Church might say or do, the fact is that kings and emperors, from Frederick II of Sicily onward, repeatedly accorded scientists their favor. Once, indeed, scientists decided to exclude theology, politics, ethics, and current events from the sphere of their discussions, they were welcomed by the heads of state. In return— and this remains one of the black marks against strict scientific orthodoxy, with its deliberate indifference to all political concerns—scientists habitually remained silent about public affairs and were outwardly, if not ostentatiously, "loyal." [26]

As the Modern Age begins, the knowledge achieved by man will no longer bow and scrape, will not apologize for itself, but claims the condition of truth. There is a growing belief that it is possible not only to know the world, but to test that knowledge, to verify it, to prove it beyond any doubt, eventually to capture in mathematical terms the absolute truth of a universal natural law. This is the eminence achieved by Newton's laws; with them the transition from the Middle Ages is over and the Modern Age is fully established.

Now, three hundred and fifty years later, Karl Popper remarks the ironic light which falls through the windows of Santa Maria sopra Minerva. No equant nor epicycle could describe a path more strange than the trajectory of the issue there joined. *Both parties have lost.* The Church has long since been driven from its claim to intimate knowledge about the nature of the universe. And the scientific heirs of Galileo have in our time stealthily withdrawn from territory they once conquered and occupied, and now speak in the unmistakable accents of Osiander and Cardinal Bellarmine. In 1927 Niels Bohr with the Principle of Complementarity renounces the attempt to make atomic theory a description of anything. The theory can be mathematically applied to certain practical ends—though we now wince at that phrase—and that is all that is claimed.

Galileo was not a martyr. Having been found guilty he read, as required, the formal abjuration which had been prepared for him; but under examination he did not recant his beliefs, he did not defend them, he denied them. Three times he was asked were it not true he had maintained that the sun stands still and the earth moves, and three times

—though he had written brilliantly in support of this proposition—he said that he had not meant what his words clearly stated. Indeed, he volunteered, if the Inquisition should wish, to write another book which would refute the Copernican system. In this confrontation over the sources of truth—in a church built on the ruins of an ancient temple of Minerva, goddess of wisdom—Galileo lied.

II

THE DREAM
OF
MECHANISM

INDETERMINACY, which we ascribe to modern physics, is our immediate and immemorial experience. Nothing is necessary, everything that happens might have happened otherwise, might never have happened at all. On adjacent sidings fast trains pause for a moment: in one a man sits in the dining car, in the other a dark-haired woman reads in her compartment, and these two places just happen to be twenty inches apart, separated by two panes of glass; the man glances up from the menu, the woman from her book, as silent forces which moved them senselessly together begin now, senselessly, to move them apart; in another moment she is gone, yet he, for having looked into the startled depths of dark eyes, will live and die a different man. A tragic and baffling contingency dogs our steps, violates our sense of order, ". . . and our lives are haunted by a Georgia slattern, because a London cutpurse went unhung." [1]

We can't abide it and so impose on visible flux a dream of hidden order. During the Middle Ages it was the will of God. Existence was regarded "as a cosmic drama," writes Carl Becker, "composed by the Master Dramatist according to a central theme and on a rational plan. Finished in idea before it was enacted in fact, before the world began written down to the last syllable of recorded time, the drama was unalterable either for good or evil." [2]

In the Modern Age the will of God is replaced by the dream of mechanism. The belief that man by his own reason can know the universe is necessarily accompanied by a changed vision of that universe. "Nature is constrained," wrote Leonardo da Vinci, "by the rational order of law which lives infused in her." No longer are natural processes subject to divine intervention. "No testimony is sufficient to establish a miracle," wrote David Hume, "unless the testimony be of such a kind that its falsehood would be more miraculous than the fact which it endeavors to establish: and even in that case there is a mutual destruction of arguments, and the superior only gives us an assurance suitable to that degree of force which remains after deducting the inferior." [3] No doubt God created the world and the firmament and set them moving, but at the beginning of the Modern Age they are seen to function independently as a machine.

The Ionian philosophers had created a model of the universe with wheels of fire in the sky; Aristotle imagined nine concentric crystalline spheres, Ptolemy thirty-nine wheels moving on wheels. These models, however, were contrivances rather than mechanisms, carried no sense of independent function, did not diminish the need for God as explanatory principle, served rather to display the inadequacy of man's reason to fathom God's plan. They were concerned with formal design, with a priori conceptions of perfect motion. Wheels and spheres rotated not in a physical but in a geometric sense; causality was left to God.

The vision of the universe as a mechanism which functions independently and lawfully according to purely physical cause first appears at the beginning of the Modern Age. "My aim," Kepler wrote,

is to show that the heavenly machine is not a kind of divine, live being, but a kind of clockwork (and he who believes that a clock has a soul, attributes the maker's glory to the work), insofar as nearly all the manifold motions are caused by a most simple, magnetic, and material force, just as all motions of the clock are caused by simple weight. And I also show how these physical causes are to be given numerical and geometrical expression.[4]

Sharing the vision that the world is knowable, the founders of the Modern Age gave voice, almost in unison, to a shared insight into method: the secrets of the universe are written in the language of mathematics; he who would know these secrets must address the universe in this language. "As the ear is made to perceive sound, and the eye to perceive color," wrote Kepler, "so the mind has been formed to understand, not all sorts of things, but quantities. It perceives any given thing more clearly in proportion as that thing is close to bare quantities as to its origin, but the further a thing recedes from quantities the more darkness and error inhere in it." [5] "Philosophy is written in this great book, the Universe," wrote Galileo,

which stands continually open to our gaze. But the book cannot be understood unless one first learns to comprehend the language and to read the letters of which it is composed. It is written in the language of mathematics, and its characters are triangles, circles, and other geometric figures, without which it is humanly impossible to understand a single word of it; without these one wanders around in a dark labyrinth.[6]

To Descartes the Angel of Truth appeared personally with the message that mathematics is the only key wherewith to unlock the secrets of nature.

The world we see and touch, however, will not fit into equations; it must first be stripped bare. "By convention sweet is sweet," Democritus wrote, "by convention bitter is bitter, by convention hot is hot, by convention cold is cold, by convention color is color. But in reality there are atoms and the void. That is, the objects of sense are supposed to be real, and it is customary to regard them as such, but in truth they are not. Only the atoms and the void are real." Rarely has a philosopher lived so in advance of his time: in the fifth century B.C. he convinced no one; in the seventeenth century, at the beginning of the Modern Age, he convinced us all. Those qualities by which we know the world—heat, color, sound, taste—may be ignored, Galileo said; for they exist only in consciousness. Descartes, continuing on this path, discarded all remaining qualities except extension and motion. "When anyone tells us," he wrote, "that he sees color in a body or feels pain in one of his limbs, this is exactly the same as if he said that he there saw or felt something, of the nature of which he was entirely ignorant, or that he did not know what he saw or felt." [7] Man and all he lives by were thus excluded from reality. What remained lay before Descartes' view as a mechanism so inter-locked and unified that one mind, he thought, should be able to work out the whole system. The end of knowledge was within sight, to be achieved within one lifetime, perhaps by Descartes himself.

The worm turns, the nail rusts, the leaf falls, the girl smiles, thunder rattles the panes, the shark moves silently in the deep. Where is mechanism? Listen to the dream. From complex whole move to less complex part. Reduce! From scullery maids and surfs and beaches, hover of hummingbirds, from pots and pans and salt and tobacco and the chatter of squirrels, from the infinity of unique instances look to the millions of substances, then to the thousands of compounds, then to the tens of elements, finally to the one elementary particle. This line moves from multiplicity to uniformity, from transience to per-manence, hence from appearance to reality, above all from randomness to lawfulness; for this final indi-visible speck doesn't smell, doesn't taste, doesn't wiggle away or wave in the wind; it has only mass and motion, and the great globe itself and all that it inherit is composed of such particles, identical each with the other; and nothing is contingent, nothing undetermined, for they move according to law. Uniform particles attract and repel, the magnitude of force being an inverse function of the square of the distance; the ultimate comprehensibility of any phenomenon depends upon its reduction to these conditions.

"Look around the world," says Cleanthes in Hume's *Dialogues Concerning Natural Religion;*

Contemplate the whole and every part of it: You will find it to be nothing but one great machine, subdivided into an infinite number of lesser machines, which again admit of subdivisions, to a degree beyond what human senses and faculties can trace and explain. All these various machines, and even their most minute parts, are adjusted to each other with an accuracy, which ravishes into admiration all men who have ever contemplated them.[8]

Laplace, sleeping on the graves of his predecessors, feverishly dreams the dream to its ultimate conclusion:

An intelligence knowing, at a given instant of time, all forces acting in nature, as well as the momentary positions of all things of which the universe consists, would be able to comprehend the motions of the largest bodies of the world and those of the smallest atoms in one single formula, provided it were sufficiently powerful to subject the data to analysis. To it, nothing would be uncertain, both future and past would be present before its eyes.[9]

Returning to the level of daily life, which now seems less real, we accept that the vision is never completely to be achieved, that we can never know exactly where the bird will alight, the arrow fall; but we take comfort, the obscure comfort of unfree men, in "knowing" that in principle it is possible, that nothing which happens could happen other than it did and does and will happen. The task of the scientist, therefore, is to reduce and simplify experience in order to discover the laws of nature which obtain at the level at which he works. The more such laws he discovers, the better will he understand and control events.

The works of Copernicus, Kepler, and Galileo were quivering fragments, alive with hidden relatedness. In Newton's hands they came together in solid interlock, revealed a coherent cosmic order governed by law—exact, permitting of no exception, given in the language of mathematics. The vision was not offered by God, but achieved by man. Man fumbled, made mistakes, false starts, but persevered. No one held his hand, no one showed the way, he got there on his own. Man can know the world. The Modern Age spreads its glittering vista, Faust begins his meteoric career.

Since nature is a mechanism, perhaps there is a natural order also for society, a right way for men to live together. Newton's success in discovering nature's laws led to the hope that laws of society—from

which man had strayed in ignorance and error—
might also be found, might then provide the basis on
which a just society could be built. The Philosophes
claimed social facts as legitimate objects of science,
confident on Cartesian authority that within the di-
versity of custom lay certain clear and simple principles which, if they could be discovered and set forth
plainly, all men of good sense would recognize.
"Even though that which in one region is called virtue," wrote Voltaire, "is precisely that which in another is called vice, even though most rules regard-
ing good and bad are as variable as the languages
one speaks and the clothing one wears; nevertheless
it seems to me certain there are natural laws with respect to which human beings in all parts of the
world must agree." [10] "Laws are the necessary relations which derive from the nature of things," wrote
Montesquieu;

and in this sense, all beings have their laws: the divinity
has its laws, the material world its laws . . . man has
his laws. Those who have said that a blind fatality has
produced all the effects that we see in the world have
uttered the great absurdity; for what greater absurdity
than a blind fatality which has produced intelligent
beings. Therefore, there is an original reason; and laws
are the relations which are found between it and different beings, and the relations of these beings among
themselves.[11]

Montesquieu, and later Locke, proceeded to "discover" and formulate these laws—balance of powers
between king, aristocracy, and the people; separa-

tion of executive, legislative, and judicial functions —and to them man began to ascribe some of that same certainty that attached to Newton's laws. "We hold these truths to be self-evident," wrote Jefferson, "that all men are created equal, that they are endowed by their Creator with certain unalienable Rights, that among these are Life, Liberty and the Pursuit of Happiness. —That to secure these rights Governments are instituted among Men, deriving their just powers from the consent of the governed."

Adam Smith, anticipating Marx, perceived historical change to issue from motives remote from any concern with the changes they were bringing about. "Human society," he wrote, "when we contemplate it in a certain abstract and philosophical light, appears like a great, an immense machine whose regular and harmonious movements produce a thousand agreeable effects." Feudal society, he believed, came to an end because feudal lords exchanged their surplus produce for the luxuries produced by the towns. "A revolution of the greatest importance to the public happiness," he wrote in *The Wealth of Nations*,

was in this manner brought about by two different orders of people who had not the least intention to serve the public. To gratify the most childish vanity was the sole motive of the great proprietors. The merchants and artificers, much less ridiculous, acted merely from a view to their own interest, and in pursuit of their own peddlar principles of turning a penny wherever a penny was to be got. Neither of them had either knowledge or foresight of that great revolution which the folly of the one, and the industry of the other, was gradually bringing about.

As human nature and social institutions were thus incorporated in the great clock, intentions became less important. The prudent investor "is led as though by an invisible hand to promote an end which is no part of his intention." "It is not from the benevolence of the butcher, the brewer, or the baker," Smith argues, "that we expect our dinner, but from their regard of their own interest. We address ourselves not to their humanity, but to their self love, and never talk to them of our own necessities, but of their advantage." Since the social machine proceeds thus inexorably and inscrutably upon its own beneficent course, human intentions were freed of moral restraint, and cupidity could indulge itself with a sense of self-righteousness, assuming that the long-range effect would be social advantage.

The medieval social order, derived from God in the ninth sphere above earth, extended in unbroken stratification through heavenly hosts to God's deputies, Emperor and Pope, thereon down through the noble orders to all lesser men, to the beasts of the field, down to non-living things, to the smallest and lowliest bit of creation, and further down to the final end point, the blackest depths of hell. This richly diversified cosmos was unified by divine revelation, and visibly symbolized at every turn and juncture of life, at every wayside and road crossing, with every ringing of the ever-ringing bells. As this social order was fragmented the various activities of man became ends in themselves, no longer accountable to God, no longer under constraint to find their proper place in the divinely ordered scheme of things. Political activity, Machiavelli perceived, is accountable only to the state and its needs. The pursuit of knowledge, as all modern philosophers agreed, is accountable only to its own rational and empirical standards. Commerce, exploration, conquest—in all these areas, man defines his own goals, pursues them as he will. "As the old sense of limitation was sundered," writes Romano Guardini,

man lost that value given those unique historical "moments" wherein the medieval belief in order had reposed. Gone was the beginning and the end, the limit and the center. The concept of hierarchy faded; with it disappeared not only all related convictions about the nature of culture but also its many symbolic accretions. The new world seemed a fabric woven of innumerable parts, a fabric which expanded in all directions. Even as this new world affirmed a freedom of space it denied to human existence its own proper place. While gaining infinite scope for movement man lost his own position in the realm of being. . . . For Dante, Ulysses had been guilty of a crime and a transgression when he sailed beyond the pillars of Gibraltar into the open sea. His act led to his destruction. For the new man of the Modern Age the unexplored regions of his world were a challenge to meet and conquer. Within himself he heard the call to venture over what seemed an endless earth, to make himself its master.[12]

For the material world the lost medieval order was replaced by the vision of mechanism; for the social life of man, the "natural laws" and "self-evident truths" postulated by Montesquieu and Locke, by Adam Smith and Jefferson, were poor substitutes for the lost hierarchy in which each person had his proper place and aim and function. The new social order strove toward a *laissez faire* in which every man would be guaranteed the freedom to pursue happiness wherever he might find it, in whatever form he might perceive it, without regard for his qualification to judge in such matters.

Modern man condemns the medieval acceptance of authority, Guardini writes,

not merely because he enjoys the discovery of autonomous investigation but because he resents the Middle Ages. His resentment is born of the realization that his own age has made revolution a perpetual institution. But authority is needed by . . . every man, even the most mature. Integral to the full grandeur of human dignity, authority is not merely the refuge of the weak; its destruction always breeds its burlesque—force. As long as medieval man was gripped by his own vision of existence, as long as he heard its music sounding in the depths of his heart, he never experienced authority as shackling. It was a bridge leading to the absolute; it was the flag of the world. Authority provided medieval man with the opportunity to construct an order whose magnificence of form, intensity of manner and richness of life were such that he would have judged our world as paltry.[13]

Scientific attitudes in the hands of philosophers harden into metaphysics.[14] Beginning with Galileo there was a strong tendency to find mechanical explanations, thereby progressively to establish the reasonableness of assuming an immutable causal order. When this "new attitude became established," wrote T. E. Hulme, "men sought to make it seem objective and necessary by giving it a philosophical setting. . . . People who are under the influence of a 'Weltanschauung' want to *fix* it, to make it seem not so much a particular *attitude* as a *necessary* fact. They then endeavor, by expressing it in a metaphysic, to give it a universal validity." [15]

Newton, by establishing the mechanics of the solar system, did more than anyone else to establish the credibility of a mechanical view of everything. "I wish we could derive the rest of the phenomena of nature," he wrote, "by the same kind of reasoning from mechanical principles." [16] He was not, however, completely committed to mechanism, felt that divine intervention might from time to time be necessary to put things back into perfect working order because, he wrote, of some "irregularities which may have arisen from the mutual actions of comets and planets upon one another, and which will be apt to increase, till this system wants a reformation." [17] Laplace was able to account mathematically for the presumed irregularities, and the mechanical model became increasingly credible. In Kant's hands a few years later causality became a priori, one of the conditions of experience and therefore not accessible to criticism on the basis of experience. This metaphysic, which followed upon and gave ideal form to a scientific climate of opinion and so was a kind of cornice to Newton's temple, was thereby given the status of a foundation.

In the course of time the metaphysic became dogma. Scientists, it was believed, could work only on the assumption that nature in all its manifestations obeys laws. Eventually the "mere fact that he is a scientist," writes Bridgman, "means that he 'believes' or 'has faith' that there are laws of nature." [18] So the supposition of mechanism becomes prescriptive and is itself removed from scientific consideration—in very much the same manner in which God's authorship of the universe was the unexamined prescriptive dogma of the Middle Ages. For two hundred and fifty years the dream of mechanism has been identified with reason, progress, enlightenment; opposition to it, with ignorance and reaction.

Precisely because a scientist talks so much about hypotheses, he is able when talking about facts to sneak in an unconscionable amount of certainty. "I am so skeptical of every assertion," he tells us, "so likely to find uncertainty in even the best-established theory, so inclined to hold back truth, to keep it tentative, that you may leave your doubts with me. When I say 'fact' you can be sure." So he lulls us, so we are beguiled.

Newton is constantly telling us he does not make hypotheses—meaning he has no explanation for gravitation. That's a matter for philosophers, he says; he is concerned only with fact. And what *is* the fact? Why, the law: Masses attract in proportion to the product of their masses and inversely as the square of their distance. He makes such a point of not knowing why this is so, that we fail altogether to note the conjecture which has slipped in without question, namely that it *is* so, that the universe is a machine coded to the inverse square. We come to believe that laws of nature *exist* in nature, that they reside there, silent, invisible, and eventually are *discovered* by man, whereas in fact they are *created* by man with nature sitting as model. The field of knowing is again split into knowledge and opinion. Natural law is but the new name for the same old absolute truth which in the Middle Ages was to be found in Holy Writ. Certainty is certainty, whether it issues from the Vatican or from the Lawrence Radiation Laboratory.

The dream of mechanism washed over Western thought. Humanities strove to become sciences, each science to become physics. Biology chased after chemistry, chemistry after mathematics—the ultimate destination in every field being always that final elementary particle; for, according to the theory of the sufficiency of atomic analysis, everything that happens upward in the hierarchy may be accounted for by events at this lowest level. Hobbes, dispensing with the subjective half of Descartes' dualism, believed that man, like the universe itself, is a machine. "For seeing life is but a motion of limbs," he wrote, "why may we not say, that all *automata* (engines that move themselves by springs and wheels as doth a watch) have an artificial life? For what is the *heart,* but a *spring;* and the *nerves,* but so many *strings;* and the *joints,* but so many *wheels,* giving motion to the whole body." Every event has a necessary cause, "so that all the effects that have been or shall be produced have their necessity in things antecedent." [19] No principle specific to life, therefore, need be invoked. All the poetry and passion, every flash of wit and laughter, all the temples of imagination and insight, can in principle be explained in atomic terms.

An arsonist hurls a bomb through a window of the Bank of America. Let us regard this event with the vision of the eighteenth century, inquire wherein lies causality, ask which of the antecedent conditions are both necessary and sufficient. Let us make a list.

The psychology of the arsonist, of course, his anger, his use of drugs, his derangement, all of which issue from his childhood experiences, and these in turn from the childhood experiences of his parents, and so on back; it must include the properties of plate glass and the decision of the architect seven years earlier to have a bay window instead of solid brick, which came about because of pressure from Rudolph Apfelbaum, the branch manager, who wanted to have a view of the ocean as he sat at his desk and discussed mortages; and of course the gambling losses of Jack Forsythe, a dental student, which induced him to sell amphetamine to the arsonist instead of saving it, as he had planned, for final exams; and the diarrhea of Tubby Watts, the night watchman at Consolidated Mining Supplies, which made him late for work on Wednesday, which made it possible for the arsonist to steal the dynamite . . . and the bacillus which caused the diarrhea . . . and Alfred Nobel, who discovered dynamite . . . and within moments the causality extends to include the entire past of the universe—to include, indeed, the position and velocity coordinates of every particle in the universe, and therefore, in principle, to be reducible to such coordinates. If this one event had to happen the way it did happen, then everything else that ever before happened or ever will happen is attended by equal inalterability, including every thought and every theory, including therefore this very sentence and the reader's reading of it. This is the vision of the world as a machine.

Since the objective study of things yields such a harvest of reliable information, should we not so study man himself? Viewing him for this purpose as an object? Could there be any area in which knowledge is more urgently needed? Should not the humanities adopt the experimental method, become social sciences? And might we not, with the added control this would yield, become able to reshape that intractable thing, society itself?

But when you study man he behaves differently:

he breathes fast, sweats, becomes self-conscious, then tries to hide it by a show of indifference. He behaves, in short, like an electron, and you can't tell what he would be if you weren't watching him. So perhaps he should not know an investigation is under way. A young female college student, an undergraduate interested in psychology, obtains a summer job as a research assistant. Her responsibility is "to entice college freshmen into cheating on tests while social psychologists use one-way mirrors and listening devices to study the freshmen's cheating and consequent breakdown when confronted with *their* immoral behavior." A Harvard scientist studies the potentiality for cruelty by requiring his subjects "to administer what they believe to be dangerous electric shocks to other subjects (accomplices of the experimenter) who beg not to be tortured further and who scream pitifully when they receive the shocks." [20]

And as it is better for the investigation that the "object" not know he is being studied, so certainly it is better for the subsequent reshaping that he not know he is being altered. For so perverse is man that he will likely react with resistance to the awareness that he is being controlled, even though he be assured it is for his own good.

In the late nineteenth century, on the furthermost reach of the wave, mechanism laid claim to the soul itself. The interior life accessible to introspection is a mechanistic function of the next level down, the level of unconscious drive, defense, and conflict; and soon, it may be assumed, these unconscious phenomena may themselves similarly be reduced to neurophysiology. Freud diagrammed the psychic apparatus, postulated those forces however hidden which would be required to make it tick, and developed a method which presumed to demonstrate the wheels upon wheels which had been inferred. Analysts sat behind couches, listened to free associations, explained to patients the causalities which had shaped them, and expected them then to be different from that which they had just proven to them they could not help being, untroubled by this or by that other, even more curious, matter that they too, the analysts, must be automata and could no more help construing the patient's life in the particular way they had arrived at than could the patient in accepting it or resisting it, and that indeed what might sound like a meaningful dialogue must be rather the synchronous but unrelated ticking of two clocks in the clock shop.

There were tremors to stir us. Becquerel found that atoms break down to energy, Einstein was reshaping Newton's machine into something more plastic and mysterious, but we were so long asleep that mechanism had become our reality, life itself our dream.

III

THE MAN WHO LOOKED INTO THE FUTURE

ONCE UPON A TIME there was a man who yearned toward the future. With clear vulnerable eyes he looked over present pain to misty goodness ahead. The present was a cruel and capricious wind, scraps of paper swirling around his legs, packed grimy snow at the street corner, cinder in the eye, the pretty girl clicking by on spike heels with no glance for him, furnished room, failure, facelessness. The future was a pretty girl looking up with adoration, lips parting, flesh melting in a sacrament of passion; was great discoveries to the benefit of mankind, and incidentally to his own security and fame; was acts of honor, heroism and sacrifice which would imprint upon flux and happenstance a seal of meaning. The present was contingency and death; the future was necessity and eternal life. The present was a desert across which, by ceaseless toil, he struggled toward the garden of the future.

He became a mathematician, got a job at IBM, sat at a desk, covered long rolls of paper with figures, could calculate with lightning speed. The digits were the present, their laws were the future; he struggled into the future of laws, replaced temporal digits with eternal symbols. He had great gift. From his pen flowed Greek letters, curved lines, pyramids, pictographs, curious marks; flowed with incredible speed from brain to pen, covering the paper with the score of strange wonderful music. He was relieved of tasks, given an office of his own, allowed to think at will and do nothing else; and from the strange music of his brain flowed great discoveries in quantum theory and statistics, from which IBM developed new polling methods of extraordinary accuracy. "You have given us," the President said, conferring upon him the Gold Medal of Merit, "the gift of prophecy." He looked up from his equations at the quivering jowls of the President, glanced around at the board of directors who were politely applauding, and saw that his gift was being efficiently translated into money.

He started his own company, made more discoveries, improved his methods, could predict national elections within a tenth of one percent, foretold business recessions, depressions, fluctuations in the price of gold. One evening toward the end of a long market slump he was able to predict that the Dow Jones average would jump fifteen points the next day, forty-five more by the end of the week, and this certainly was good news for the country at large, but the fact that he knew it first, it occurred to him, could be even better news for him personally. He borrowed fifty thousand dollars, bought Xerox on margin.

People trusted him. So successful he became that his own predictions became factors to reckon with in his total calculations. If he found that Industrials would jump ten points, then that prediction itself would cause another rise of four—to a total of fourteen. His equations became more complicated, began to correct themselves: any particular equation, arrived at by *him*, became a quantity of force altering the aggregates of forces being equated. So his calculations became self-conscious, the strange music of his pen began to listen to its own melody, to make corrections in its own intensity, even at times to change its theme. Many political candidates, in fact, would decide, months in advance of announcing their candidacy, not to run, conceding defeat in some phantom election of the future which had in a sense already occurred and therefore would never take place.

The President of the United States called often, came to depend upon him. "What will it do to my popularity if I veto the fair housing bill?" "What will be the effect over a period of three months on the number of registered Democrats in Dutchess County if I step up the bombing fifteen percent?" "Dear friend," the President said one day with tears in his eyes, "I really couldn't do without you. You're my right arm." "Think nothing of it," said the mathematician, and upped his fee another hundred thousand dollars. He developed the largest polling service in the world with offices in every county in the United States and every country of the world.

As he became more famous and more wealthy he noticed a curious trend in his life: the more he could see into the future the more he lived in the present. Formerly he had filled the present with drudgery, located all pleasure in the future. Now it was turning the other way around. All right, he thought, I'll try it, will go all the way. The first half of my life was given to the future, the rest I'll give to the present, will make no commitment to anyone or anything. He stopped working, didn't have to, his organization could run itself. Leases on his patents brought in floods of money. He sighed happily, resigned himself to a life of pleasure—girls, gambling, auto racing, gourmet food.

Gradually having fun became a strain, he had to work at it, and the time came finally when he could no longer conceal this from himself. "I can't bear doing just what I want to do," he said, "I'll go crazy." But he was crazy anyway, he knew, because what better thing could he do than what he wanted to do? This is a problem, he said, and got out his slide rule and pencil and paper. "Let a represent any value. Then perhaps it may be said that a cannot exist alone, but only in relation to $b, c, d. \ . \ . \ .$ Everything, that is, has to be validated by something else, and a present for which no future vouches is worthless."

This hypothesis he found unpleasant, even sinister, for it would push him right back where he came from, toward a commitment to the future. He strug-

gled against it. "I don't want to live that way," he
said. "I've had it, it's no good, it's a waiting, a fast,
and I want to feast, now, now, now!" So he tried
even harder. The eating of delicate delicious food,
he thought, surely that must be a value in itself,
something that can stand against any nihilism. He
tried, became a habitué of the great restaurants of
the world, but found that the eating of food wants to
serve the morrow, that when the morrow it serves
contains nothing more than eating, that food itself
becomes dust. In the Tour d'Argent he pondered
this matter, looked out unseeing over Notre Dame,
brooded on the crystalline evening, pulled his eye-
brows, while before him appeared, successively,
*Croustades aux Truffes, Vol au Vent aux Quenelles
de Brochet, Poitrine de Veau Farcie, Endives au
Gratin*—each served with great flourish, allowed to
grow cold, sorrowfully removed. When finally the
Soufflé au Chocolat Flambé collapsed untouched the
kitchen door splintered and the chef, as if fired from
a cannon, hurled himself upon the reluctant diner,
threw all the dishes on the floor, smashed the table,
and had to be hospitalized. In the Four Seasons he
looked out over a smoky red Manhattan sunset, did
not notice the *Pintade au Genièvre* nor realize that
the man in black tie who had sat down beside him
and was weeping in a napkin was the Maître d'.

But orgasm, he thought, now there's a thing in itself, the supreme value, perhaps the only one that
can stand alone, needing no validation. He polled
the model agencies, gathered together the most beau-
tiful girls in the world. It didn't work. He became

frantic, tried two at a time, then a whole roomful, but it failed. Orgasm, he found, is a jewel which, the more it glitters, the more it cries out for a setting of love, lacking which the sparkle is lost and the jewel falls unnoticed to the floor. But love lays claim to the future, commits the present to the securing of that future.

So the present turned to dust. Very well, he thought, I'll go back to my old ways, will tie myself to the future. The present will acquire value relative to future goods. But the future now seemed dismal, boring, without good. He scratched frantically, but all he could find in the future was more of the present—wars, depressions, labor disputes, revolutions, counterrevolutions, hurricanes, airplane crashes, people being born, people dying. As for the market—it would continue to fluctuate. The more clearly the future could be seen, the more evident that it could validate nothing.

He had painted himself into a corner. Sensuality, referring to nothing beyond the senses, had become boredom. On gourmet meals he had become not fat, but quite thin. And though he still bedded girls on occasion it was with a hidden elegiac asceticism, as if looking for God. Through temples of pleasure he wandered, untempted, out into the desert to draw faces in the sand.

The vision is lost. Even if the world *were* a machine, if Bohr, Heisenberg, and Born were mistaken, and if quantum events could be reduced to predictable occurrence by formula—even then the causal view is lost. Mathematics itself precludes that final crystalline clarity for which mathematics has for centuries been the symbol. For if the cosmos *were* a machine, everything within that cosmos—shoes and ships, cabbages and countesses and worms, the mind of man and every last thought and theory and feeling of man—would be part of that machine. Therefore we who think about these matters and speculate on the possibly machine-like nature of the universe would be in the position of one cog on one wheel attempting to figure out whether the whole apparatus is or is not a machine. Gödel's theory, as well as quite common commonsense, indicates that this is not possible; that though the cog might formulate the problem it could not, within the machine, answer it; that since, in this case, the machine is the entire cosmos, there is not, even in principle, a way to stand outside it; that, therefore, the question cannot be answered nor the problem ever solved; and that, consequently, the supposition is idle and meaningless, like a man before a mirror asking the man he sees what the man in the mirror is asking.

IV

PURSUIT OF THE DIMINISHING OBJECT

LAWS OF NATURE may be discovered only by observing objects; but the objects we live with, being complex and multi-faceted, will not do. We can't find the arc of planets by sliding kitchen pots down drainboards: the pots are greasy, the drainboard wet, the air resistance incalculable; in such a laboratory we find only contingency and indeterminacy. The search for mechanism requires clean objects, free of influence, in order that the behavior observed may be truly ascribed to the object. To this end we isolate what we study, simplify it, break it into smaller pieces, wash it, use ever more delicate and accurate instruments, and in so doing achieve a steady gain in lawfulness: compounds behave more predictably than mixtures, elements than compounds. Proceeding on this path we reach finally the atom, but do not stop. Having become God, we know no limit; spiraling ever further downward we break the indivisible atom into electrons and protons, and now surely we have reached the smallest constituents of mechanism. Millikan, with hushed awe, describes our arrival at these tiniest jewels of the great clock:

Nothing more beautifully simplifying has ever happened in the history of science than the whole series of discoveries culminating about 1914 which finally brought practically universal acceptance to the theory that the material world contains but two fundamental entities, namely, positive and negative electrons, exactly alike in charge, but differing widely in mass, the positive electron—now usually called a proton—being 1850 times heavier than the negative, now usually called simply the electron.[1]

But we have jarred Pandora's box, and soon we have, also, neutrons, and neutrinos and positrons; and now a curious cutback occurs: the behavior of these tiny bits of matter becomes not more lawful, but less, not more predictable, but more indeterminate. Mechanism disappears at precisely that point at which we were finally going to nail it down forever. At the heart of the machine we are enveloped in mist, have lost our way, are far from home.

We become aware then that our observation is disturbing the object. We may, if we wish, assume that the electron does really *have* position and velocity though we cannot ascertain both, that it really *is* either a wave or a particle though we cannot know which, that the indeterminacy is appearance not reality—we are free so to imagine; but then must accept that we have composed a fairy tale, not a theory, for it is by definition something that cannot be tested—like saying that turtles, when completely unobserved, become princes. There is no escape; for observation of any kind whatever is an interaction between the object of knowledge and some means of gaining information about it. There is no such thing as a naked object: whatever we know is already a little different by virtue of our knowing it, clothed a bit by the questions we have asked, by the way we have sidled up to it.

"Newton left the impression," writes F. S. C. Northrop,

> that there were no assumptions in his physics which were not necessitated by the experimental data . . . that he made no hypotheses and that he had deduced his basic concepts and laws from the experimental findings. Were this conception of the relation between the physicist's experimental observations and his theory correct, Newton's theory would never have required modification. . . . Being implied by the facts, it would be as indubitable and final as they are.[2]

We know now that this is not and can never be the case, that no law of nature owes everything to nature and nothing to man, that no law is a forced deduction from empirical findings; for every law embodies not only an ordering of empirical findings but something also of the speculative and creative mind which divined that order.

The longing is deep, we cling. Does it really matter, we would ask, this craziness at the subatomic level? Is not mechanism already firmly established at higher levels? But here we turn back awkwardly on our own steps: it was precisely the indeterminacy of life as we see it and live it—in the realm of pots and pans and scullery maids, of violin cadenzas, and bombs breaking windows—that led us down that tunnel of matter in pursuit of mechanism; now, having come out in a land of chaos, we would turn back claiming the excursion was elective, the dream already well established before we set out to find it.

We don't know anything for sure, can't predict anything with certainty, not the weather tomorrow nor the election next fall nor where the bird will alight or the arrow fall, and as for that eclipse next year which we have scheduled to the hundredth of a second, a wandering asteroid may have destroyed the moon altogether by then. What happens happens, and follows from antecedent states, but whether necessarily or unnecessarily we have no dispensation to know. If an exceptionless necessity were demonstrable at the microscopic level, then such necessity could perhaps be plausibly inferred, though it could never be proved, for the macroscopic level. Lacking demonstration at any level, the inference is gratuitous; and our holy mission to get it all straight has yielded an ever proliferating brood of erratically behaving elementary particles, each of which is composed of elementary particles. "The conception of objective reality," writes Heisenberg, "has thus evaporated . . . into the transparent clarity of a mathematics that represents no longer the behavior of particles but rather our knowledge of this behavior." [3]

The only interpretation of the new facts, Bridgman writes,

is that our conviction that nature is understandable and subject to law arose from the narrowness of our horizons, and that if we would sufficiently extend our range we shall find that nature is intrinsically and in its elements neither understandable nor subject to law. . . . The precise reason that the law of cause and effect fails can be paradoxically stated; it is not that the future is not determined in terms of a complete description of the present, but that in the nature of things the present cannot be completely described. . . . The world is not a world of reason, understandable by the intellect of man, but as we penetrate ever deeper, the very law of cause and effect, which we had thought to be a formula to which we could force God Himself to subscribe, ceases to have a meaning.[4]

Already in the nineteenth century it had been found that field phenomena cannot be reduced to mechanics. But by then the wheels and gears were inside our heads. "I am never content," writes Lord Kelvin as late as 1884, "until I have constructed a mechanical model of the object I am studying. If I succeed in making one, I understand; otherwise I do not. Hence I cannot grasp the electromagnetic theory of light. I wish to understand light as fully as possible, without introducing things that I understand still less." [5]

At the same time the humanities, straining desperately to be sciences and always lagging, were entering their most mechanistic phase. Biology with Darwin, sociology with Marx, psychology with

Freud, all saw the hidden machine, all strove to reduce variety of experience to unity of principle, apparent newness to hidden recurrence, the unforeseeable to the inevitable, appearance to reality. "The chaotic universe of change," Barzun writes, referring to Darwin and to Marx,

> was made rational by the ordinary fact of struggle; the anarchy of social existence was organized around class hatred. . . . The beholder began with a matter of fact and could reach symbolism and true knowledge with only an effort of application and memory. Physical struggle led to survival, physical labor to value . . . and at the end of each system yielded the most exalted objects of contemplation; the adaptation of living form; a perfect state. . . .[6]

In mechanism, writes Whitehead, "the world had got hold of a general idea which it could neither live with nor live without." [7] "The misfortune," Barzun writes, "was that when mechanism began to be questioned, for scientific reasons, the general public had become persuaded of its absolute truth; it could think in no other terms and it felt that all other views were simply 'prescientific.' " [8]

Experimental physics cannot deal with the arsonist, has nothing to say about the contingency or inevitability of his behavior. The philosophy of mechanism *assumes* inevitability, and would wish to give force to this assumption by proving mechanism at the microscopic level. But what gets established when the cosmos is observed with very high magnification is indeterminacy and graininess. "When a slender beam of light is passed through a system of slits," writes Bridgman,

the pattern ordinarily seen is . . . light and dark bands with smooth gradations from light to dark. But if the intensity of light is made very low, the smooth pattern breaks down into a pattern of individual spots, which mark the arrival of individual photons of light and the excitation of individual grains of the photographic emulsion. The place and time of occurrence of any individual spot in this pattern are at present absolutely unpredictable.

It is not, however, necessary, he adds, that this unpredictable event have only microscopic consequences, for "it would be possible so to couple a disintegrating speck of some radioactive compound to an atomic bomb as to blow up a city at an absolutely unpredictable time." [9] Likewise, we would add, the arrival of that photon at one point rather than another within the nucleus of one brain cell might achieve an equal extension of effect, perhaps sufficient to make the difference between the arsonist's hurling of the bomb or his dropping it in the gutter.

Descartes convinced us that the world is comprised of two entities, mind which has the property of consciousness and matter which has the property of extension. Mind is aloof from matter, cannot be touched by it or affected. Here begins our scientific objectivity, the vision of the knower and the known, intimately related, sailing through eternity together, yet occupying different realms, independent, not touching. Mind may thereby regard itself as an alien spirit, invisible, weightless, moving about freely in the world of things, observing, contriving, devising, inferring, deducing, and so coming to know the extended world, formulating its laws in the language of mathematics, without itself affecting material things or being affected by them. This is the famous Cartesian clarity. Let us look more closely.

There really are three substances; for we need God as connecting medium between the other two. The soul lives in the pineal gland; in this bit of tissue at the base of the skull the three come uneasily together. Since matter can have no effect on mind it is difficult to account for why the mind feels "sorrow" when the body feels "thirst." Mind cannot cause anything to move or stop anything from moving, since the total quantity of motion in the universe is eternally fixed, but can change the direction of motion. But if the motion the direction of which is altered happens to be the point of a sword, might it not come about consequent to that deflection that the blade transfixes the heart of a man it otherwise would have missed? And might this not affect the pineal gland connected with that heart, to the end that the soul which lived there and is now made homeless may be said to have been profoundly affected by matter?

Descartes' Dutch disciple Geulincx proceeded to iron out these wrinkles by a final complete separation: mind cannot affect matter in any way, and matter cannot affect mind. Isn't it curious, though, that my hand moves immediately after my mind conceives the wish that it move? And not only curious, but fortunate; for otherwise my hand would be carrying food to my mouth and stuffing it down when I had no wish to eat but would rather be talking. This difficulty, however, is easily dispelled by the theory of the two clocks: not only are mind and matter irrevocably separate, they are also perfectly synchronized. "Suppose you have two clocks," Bertrand Russell explains,

which both keep perfect time: whenever one points to the hour, the other will strike, so that if you saw one and heard the other you would think the one *caused* the other to strike. So it is with mind and body. Each is wound up by God to keep time with the other, so that, on occasion of my volition, purely physical laws cause my arm to move, although my will has not really acted on my body.[10]

Step by step the clarity becomes more awesome, but soon the shadows in Plato's cave have more reality.

We blame nothing on Descartes. He but proposes; it is we who concur. And what we have done, at his suggestion, is to flay the sensuous world, strip away the green leaves, the taste of strawberry, the smell of rose, the haze on the hills in October, the feel of a girl's mouth. We stride across the world like a god, jettison most of what we see. It's not real, and we have no time for appearance. We must strike to the heart of matter. So little do we retain of the sensible world—extension and motion—but must be consoled for the impoverishment of experience, we are told, by knowing that these primary qualities, being objective and imperishable, will never desert us.

Now life takes revenge, with savage aptness snatches from our hands these last two qualities. We have sacrificed the world for nothing. Along comes the gentle Einstein in baggy pants, with soulful eyes and uncut hair, and takes away not only extension, but also that time by which we set such store. There are two parties, he reminds us, to every observation, the observer as well as the observed. And where should the observer stand to get an accurate view of those primary, objective, and imperishable qualities? It turns out there is no *right* place to stand, no place at all, in fact, which we can know is at rest. Measuring rods collapse, miles shrink down to inches, clocks are frozen in ancient ice; an eternity may elapse between this sip of coffee and the next, and we shall never know.

Where now is that sensuous world we so arrogantly dismissed? Where is that haze on the hills in October and the smell of burning leaves, the taste of strawberries, the touch of lips? Is it too late? May we still go home again?

The rising importance of the concept of causality means the development in man of a steadily increasing tendency to look but briefly at the thing itself, then quickly to its antecedents, the conditions and influences from which it may have been derived. The hypnotic fascination with causality turns our heads, we look backwards. So the past is augmented at the expense of the present. History is born, and soon, as Becker writes, "historical-mindedness is so much a preconception of modern thought that we can identify a particular thing only by pointing to the various things it successively was before it became that particular thing which it will presently cease to be." [11] "We explain things by their origins," writes Barzun, "take conditions for causes, and cannot resist the lure of profundity. The *surface* of things, their *present* state, their interpretation by consequences instead of antecedents—all leave us intellectually at sea." [12]

E. A. Burtt traces the historical change in our thinking about causes—from the teleological causality of the Medieval Age to the mechanistic causality of the Modern Age to our present preference for an evolutionary causality. "Now it is a possible hypothesis at least," he writes,

that so far as the data of science are concerned we are left undetermined as between these assumptions of what constitutes an adequate causal explanation, and that the factors conditioning a selection between them are to be found primarily in we who think about the world rather than the world we are thinking about. Perhaps it is the rise to a dominating ambition of the human need to control nature's processes, and to do so as exactly as possible, that accounts for our modern preferences in this matter.[13]

We have attention, curiosity, creativity, in but limited amount; in the Modern Age a large part of this vital force is withdrawn from the trembling leaf, from the smell of a rose, from the mouth of a girl, from the dancing feet. In the interest of power we are forever looking back, picking among the ruins for causes. We would rather control the world than experience it, to this end will sacrifice anything, everything, life itself.

Tennyson in *In Memoriam* invokes a priestess from the vaults of death, implores her for a revelation: " 'The stars,' she whispers, 'blindly run.' " "This line," Whitehead writes,

states starkly the whole philosophic problem. . . . Each molecule blindly runs. The human body is a collection of molecules. Therefore, the human body blindly runs, and therefore there can be no individual responsibility for the actions of the body. If you once accept that the molecule is definitely determined to be what it is, independently of any determination by reason of the total organism of the body, and if you further admit that the blind run is settled by the general mechanical laws, there can be no escape from this conclusion.

He cites the view of John Stuart Mill that

volitions are determined by motives, and motives are expressible in terms of antecedent conditions including states of mind as well as states of body. . . . [This] doctrine is generally accepted, especially among scientists, as though in some way it allowed you to accept the extreme doctrine of materialistic mechanism, and yet mitigated its unbelievable consequences. It does nothing of the sort. Either the bodily molecules blindly run, or they do not. If they do blindly run, the mental states are irrevelant in discussing the bodily actions.

"A scientific realism based on mechanism," he writes, in another context,

is conjoined with an unwavering belief in the world of men and of the higher animals as being composed of self-determining organisms. This radical inconsistency at the basis of modern thought accounts for much that is half-hearted and wavering in our civilization. . . . The men of the Middle Ages were in pursuit of an excellency of which we have nearly forgotten the existence. They set before themselves the ideal of the attainment of a harmony of the understanding. We are content with superficial orderings from diverse arbitrary starting points.[14]

Although the medieval world was limited in extension, Guardini writes, "the finiteness of the world . . . was balanced, so to speak, by an infinity in depth. This it gained by the symbolic meaning which shone through the whole of reality." [15]

If every event follows necessarily from some antecedent state, then the cosmos is a machine. But if some events do not follow necessarily from any antecedent state, then the cosmos is not a machine, the occurrence or non-occurrence of such events cannot be reduced to law, and the universe is never to be known completely. The breakdown of mechanism, therefore, breaks our vision of the world as knowable. It is fitting that physics, that most scientific of sciences, so largely responsible for the birth of the modern world, should officiate so expertly at its obsequies.

"But what physicists have learned from the history of their science," Barzun writes, "has not yet been learned by the biologists, which accounts for the curious fact that while some physicists are becoming a new sort of 'vitalist,' most biologists are still for the most part, mechanists—like the ordinary man." [16]

In the noonday of Newton's universe it was taken as self-evident that reasoning by induction leads to general law, and the philosophic problem was to understand how the examination of special cases could lead to general truths. Now, in the twilight, it is known that reasoning by induction leads only to propositions of greater or lesser likelihood, and the concern of philosophers is with the nature of probability.[17] In Newtonian mechanics inaccuracies of measurement are independent of each other and may be reduced to negligibility; in quantum mechanics inaccuracies of measurement are reciprocally related and, though the uncertainty may in principle be reduced to Planck's constant, this is not for atomic particles negligible. This little h sneers at Laplace's demon. Man's presumption has led him down a trail of triumphs in knowing to an abyss of uncertainty.

We associate the breakup of mechanism with discoveries of the twentieth century, but the model was flawed from the outset, and fatally. For he who says the universe is a mechanism is that same Cretan who told us all Cretans were liars. For if man and all his works, his vision and insight, be excepted from mechanism, then the theory is thereby revised, and one is saying rather that part of the universe is a mechanism; and then, clearly, it becomes possible that the part which is not mechanical may act unpredictably upon the part which is, to the end that no part is reliably mechanical. If the universe is one great clock, that's one thing; but if it is a great clock plus a curious demon, that's quite a different matter, for who knows when the demon may take a notion to oil it or throw in a bit of sand? Moreover, if man be excepted from the mechanism, what reasonable basis could exist for assuming that he is the only exception?

If, on the other hand, man and all his genius, his theories, his wonder, his works of art, are an intrinsic component of the one universal mechanism—perhaps the most complex and specialized circuit of the cosmic computer, even designed, perhaps, to visualize all the other circuits—then one must accept that the vision of mechanism is itself as completely determined as everything else, could not occur otherwise, could not fail to occur, and that any critical discussion about its truth is the rustle of wind in dry grass.

We have followed a dream of objective truth, have reached out toward something knowable which, being known, will yet remain independent of the knowing process and of the knowing mind, unaffected by the questions it asks, the wonder it feels, the picking up, the pulling and pushing, the getting close. We know there is something out there—a star perhaps or an atom, maybe a butterfly, a piece of cheese, a pretty girl—something . . . something real, with which we are in contact, interaction, about which we can formulate statements. From the darkness inside our skulls we lean toward it, believing that sometimes when we are both fortunate and diligent one of our statements may achieve such perfect correspondence to that reality that the content and configuration of the statement will in no way derive from the questions asked, or from the questioner, or the methods used, but will owe everything to the known; and that therefore, given a sufficient capacity for knowing, anybody in this world, or in any other world, in any age, would arrive at exactly the same formulation.

But the reality seized by the statement is already different by virtue of being so taken, and the statement itself bears trace of the hand and mind which did the seizing. "The syllogism," writes Bridgman, ". . . demands that we be able to say the same thing twice. But we can never say anything *exactly* the same twice, for we as living, or indeed as material, creatures are involved in the inexorable irreversible process of the entire universe. The 'sameness' on repetition can therefore be only an approximate sameness, and logic cannot be completely sharp." [18]

Descartes drove such a wedge between thought

and nature that, for three hundred years, we have studied nature as if thought, running parallel—and the life of the thinker with its sorrows and vanities, nights of ecstasy, nights of fear—did not influence what we observed, did not participate in what we found. We have presumed ourselves outside of nature, like the mind of God, looking in. Officially we deny it, are loud on our oneness with nature, but it has a forced quality, deceives no one, like the muffled reply of the thief in the chickenhouse: "Nobody here, Boss, but us chickens."

Who are we to claim objectivity? We are the interested judge, we hold stock in this corporation. And have we not, moreover, known it all along? Has not our seeming unawareness been designed to retain for us, if challenged, the right to claim inadvertence? Now indeed we *are* challenged and the inadvertence is not credible. We had hoped, if we just kept quiet, that it would go away, that no one would notice. We have come a long way on false credentials; now our time of arrogance is coming to an end. We are not entitled to grace in getting out, to peace with honor; we're being driven and had better hurry. Unless we acknowledge our compromised position and disqualify ourselves as judge we shall be hauled down from the bench and beaten to our knees with weapons of our own presumption.

We have lost the division between subject and object, are left with a field of knowing in which object partakes of subject. From hovering helicopter we shoot the fleeing polar bear and, while he is stunned, tag him; and, finding him again next year, we "know" something about the migration of polar bears. But the bear we know has had the encounter, has suffered the poisoned dart, and so may have roamed a different floe, drifted in different currents. Whatever we know of anything has come to be known, not only by our perceptions and our measurements, but also by our questions which derive from what we are and what we believe—things which change with time. Another type of being with different preconceptions addressing itself to the same phenomenon would arrive at different knowledge.

The knower, likewise, is changed by the known. We may never forget that polar bear, the terror and hate on his face, the frantic scampering to escape the clatter of the helicopter, the wash of the blades, the merciless trajectory of the dart; and the memory may change us, may lead us one day years later to befriend a wounded raccoon, to take him home, not knowing he has rabies, where he bites the thumb of a gifted pianist, our wife's cousin, who had stopped in for tea.

The world to us is a woman in our arms; we may know her but will change her, and in being known she changes us. So we hold the world and are held by it, struggle together, are bound together inalienable, and so sail through a void forever. We should not boast of conquest—modesty better becomes our achievements in knowing—mindful that she whom we held yesterday may surprise us today with qualities born of the embrace. She's not of iron, but mutable as are we; and we may, if careless, destroy in her what most we love.

V

RELATIVITY
OF
KNOWLEDGE

EVERY AGE achieves certainty. The character of an age is determined by the source of its sureness.

As we perceive our own certainties to issue from reliable knowledge of the world, and as we look back over the great increase in such knowledge during the life of mankind, we might suppose a steady historical increase in certitude reaching in our times a sureness greater than that of any past age. Not so. Certainty derives from need rather than knowing, is always available in the amount required, and so tends to be a fixed quantity in human affairs. Every age achieves knowledge as opposed to opinion, for knowledge is the name we give to those of our opinions to which certainty is ascribed. Certainty would falter were it derived from conjecture; conjecture which leads to certainty must be labeled fact, truth, natural law.

We are enlightened and critical about the certainties of the past but are not likely even to notice our own, far less to be critical. In the Modern Age it is fashionable to advance our doubts, our tentativeness; an open mind is esteemed more highly than an informed one; the capacity to find one's self mistaken, to change, is mark of excellence. Certainty lurks, however, and many of us who disavow it might discover in ourselves certain knowledge that, for example, a democratic society is better than a dictatorship. Even so modest a thinker as John Dewey, so critical of all absolutes, lapses when discussing learning through doing, his area of special enthusiasm, into statements of unabashed certitude: "An idealism of action that is devoted to creation of a future, instead of to staking itself upon propositions about the past, is invincible." [1] Perhaps. But we would note in passing that Hitler along with other tyrants would agree, and that he—and they—proved vincible.

Whenever man addresses himself to the world and asks such questions as: What is this? How does it come about? What does it mean? he is bound to make conjectures. Some of these conjectures catch on, a chord important to the times responds, they seem to fit, are held as truth, often as self-evident truth, and gather to themselves various kinds of authority—institutional, mystical, scientific, religious. They may become the eternal verities of their time, and it will then seem inconceivable to those who hold them that they should ever fall in doubt. Everything under the moon is subject to generation and to decay, said Aristotle, whereas everything above the moon, being composed of a divine element, is unchanging and indestructible; for fifteen hundred years this dictum was absolute truth. Similar certainty has attended the divine right of kings, ordeal by water, the evil of witches.

Since man became a historical being each age has been able to recognize the certainties of the past as mistaken, often as absurd. Eternal verities prove both transient and untrue. We look back and see that they were held by a particular people with unique mores living on a limited segment of earth during a certain period of time, and that whatever apparent validity they had was bound to those circumstances. What was self-evident truth to them is seen by us to be arbitrary, culturally relative, derived from needs and fears.

As historical consciousness lengthens, more layers of the past can be examined and compared. It becomes possible for a certain age, A, to look back to an earlier age, B, and to observe that B, in writing the history of a still earlier age, C, recognizes (correctly, we believe) the cherished beliefs of C as primitive superstitions, whereas B's cherished beliefs are seen by B as enlightened and rational, indeed not as beliefs at all, but as objective findings, self-evident truths. But A, in considering B's beliefs, alleged to be so rational and enlightened, finds them just as mistaken, though perhaps in a different direction, as C's.

Such findings pose a special problem: If at every level of the past, eternal verities are found to be culturally relative, must we not infer likewise for our own? Must we not accept for our own fundamental truths that our firm belief, even our readiness to die for them, is evidential of nothing? that all past ages felt likewise about their truths which came in time to seem so in error? Must we not then give up the hope to know the world, accept the likelihood that none of our information is reliable, that nothing is certain?

Descartes had little use for opinion, was in life-long pursuit of hard data. "Seeing how many different opinions are sustained by learned men about one item," he writes, "without its being possible for more than one ever to be true, I took to be tantamount to false everything which was merely probable." Early in life he discovered that most of the truths from the past are false. "I was brought up from childhood on letters," he relates,

and, because I had been led to believe that by this means one could acquire clear and positive knowledge of everything useful in life, I was extremely anxious to learn them. But, as soon as I had completed this whole course of study, at the end of which it is usual to be received into the ranks of the learned, I completely changed my opinion. For I was assailed by so many doubts and errors that the only profit I appeared to have drawn from trying to become educated, was progressively to have discovered my ignorance. And yet I was at one of the most famous schools in Europe.

He had the courage of his misgivings, concluded "that there was no body of knowledge in the world such as [he] had been led previously to believe existed." [2]

How avoid the endless repetition of this pattern? How think now such that one's thought in a thousand years will not itself be exhibited in some showcase of superstition or intellectual oddity? The only safeguard, Descartes finds, is a method of systematic doubt: nothing must be accepted on faith or on authority, every assertion that aspires to truth must be examined with radical incredulity. "What is there, then, that can be esteemed true? Perhaps this only, that there is absolutely nothing certain." [3]

Now here is a man to follow. Let us watch him take the first step. "While I wanted to think everything false, it must necessarily be that I who thought was something; and remarking that this truth, *I think, therefore I am,* was so solid and so certain that all the most extravagant suppositions of the skeptics were incapable of upsetting it, I judged that I could receive it without scruple as the first principle of the philosophy that I sought." [4] All right so far; but, following in these footsteps, we come soon upon very strange scenery: all things that we conceive very clearly and very distinctly are true; clear *per*ception may be an illusion, but clear *con*ception is utterly trustworthy; God must exist, for no idea can be more clearly and precisely conceived; likewise he must be perfect and righteous, for if he were not then man could not trust in anything. Having so proved the existence of God, he now can prove anything; and the universe which by such steps is necessarily deduced is now to be seen, along with other specimens, in the museum of intellectual oddities:

the universe is infinitely full of matter, so densely packed that no one particle can move unless all the other particles move at the same time; whirlpools of matter are thus created which carry sun and stars in their orbits. His method of radical doubt accounts for clouds raining blood, explains how lightning may be turned into snow. Beginning with skepticism, he bequeaths us another lease on that same certainty that mankind, one way or another, has always found.

He was a small man with a large head and a large nose, curly black hair, and dark incredulous eyes set wide apart. His voice was feeble; but his words still nag at us after three hundred years, passages of great arrogance alternating with passages of excessive and unconvincing modesty. He was a shy man with quirks, liked to sleep till noon in warm rooms. Stockholm was very cold, Queen Christina had to have her lesson at five o'clock in the morning, and Descartes did not last the winter; he died of pneumonia on the 11th of February, 1650.

At the beginning of the Modern Age science began to affect life in two opposite ways, each enormously reinforcing the other: it began to expose much of what had passed for knowledge as superstition, and it began to establish new knowledge of unprecedented reliability. The organic development of human knowledge, moving sluggishly like a glacial finger in a long valley, with slow accretions and quiet losses, was suddenly fragmented. Enlightened skepticism played like a merciless searchlight over the wrinkled faces of cherished beliefs. Empiricism and experiment formed the mode of knowing, there was a demand for hard facts, and the spiritual baggage of mankind, seen now mostly as junk, began to drop by the wayside. This was the exuberant youth of the scientific revolution. A new kind of truth was afoot in the world—transcultural, transinstitutional, absolutely true yet qualitatively different from the absolute truths which issue from mores, which time inexorably falsifies. Surely the pursuit of this kind of truth, the extension of its search and its methods into all fields, is the path of progress. Now in the twilight of the Modern Age one still hears this voice: ". . . science has humanized our values," writes Bronowski. "Men have asked for freedom, justice and respect precisely as the scientific spirit has spread among them." [5]

The corpus of human knowledge was split, one part consisting of propositions derived from faith, tradition, intuition, need—for example, "We hold these truths to be self-evident, that all men are created equal, that they are endowed by their Creator with certain unalienable rights, that among these are life, liberty, and the pursuit of happiness"—the other part, of propositions derived from a newly flourishing scientific method—for example, "The pressure of a confined gas is reciprocally related to the volume, the temperature being constant." Jefferson's assertion, though perhaps true for a certain people at a certain time in their history, cannot be tested, cannot be proven, is culturally bound, cannot be guaranteed true throughout past and future. Whereas Boyle, having formulated the gas law, having tested it, verified it, might have reflected that it was as true in China as in England, that it held equally for the breath of Christ on the cross and for the wind cleft by the sword of Genghis Khan, that its truth was transcultural, timeless, and absolute. Science, therefore, achieves knowledge of great certitude, reaching at times, it was believed, the absolute truth of a mathematically formulated law, while the faiths of man, acting through tradition, achieve arbitrary knowledge without certitude, liable to be dismissed as superstition by a later generation.

As this division widens and deepens, it comes about that those beliefs deriving from faith no longer seem deserving of the status of knowledge. Their dearth of certititude relegates them to an inferior realm—arbitrary, passionate, irrational, stained by time and place, incapable of mathematical expression. The only knowledge then is science, the rest is politics. "The method of scientific investigation," wrote Thomas Huxley,

is nothing but the expression of the necessary mode of working of the human mind. It is simply the mode at which all phenomena are reasoned about, rendered precise and exact. There is no more difference, but there is just the same kind of difference, between the mental operations of a man of science and those of an ordinary person, as there is between the operations and methods of a baker or of a butcher weighing out his goods in common scales, and the operations of a chemist in performing a difficult and complex analysis by means of his balance and finely graduated weights. It is not that the action of the scales in one case, and the balance in the other, differ in the principles of their construction or manner of working; but the beam of one is set on an infinitely finer axis that the other, and of course turns by the addition of a much smaller weight.[6]

Science would have us believe that such accuracy, leading to certainty, is the only criterion of knowledge, would make the trial of Galileo the paradigm of the two points of view which aspire to truth, would suggest, that is, that the cardinals represent only superstition and repression, while Galileo represents freedom and true knowledge.

But there is another criterion which is systematically neglected in this elevation of science. Man does not now—and will not ever—live by the bread of scientific method alone. He must deal with life and death, with love and cruelty and despair, and so must make conjectures of great importance which may or may not be true and which do not lend themselves to experimentation: It is better to give than to receive; Love thy neighbor as thyself; Better to risk slavery through non-violence than to defend freedom with murder. We must deal with such propositions, must decide whether they are true, whether to believe them, whether to act on them— and scientific method is no help, for by their nature these matters lie forever beyond the realm of science. One of these crucial conjectures concerns science itself: The long-range influence of science will be for the good of mankind. This is not a scientific hypothesis the credibility of which can be established by certain crucial experiments. It is a hope, a wish, a statement of faith; it may or may not be true.

So great has been the success of scientific method that it has come to be identified with reason itself—as if there were no way of being reasonable with conjectures that lie beyond scientific reach. Such conjectures therefore are insidiously disparaged, ignored, as if to say, "If it's not scientific it's not important." This may prove to be a fatal lapse. For much scientific knowledge is of great certitude but little importance, while much traditional knowledge is of little certitude but extreme importance. To live is to act. We feel, we reflect, we experiment in laboratories—but we don't stop there. We go on to appraise issues, to make decisions, and then to move. And as we appraise and decide we make reference not only to scientific knowledge but much more extensively to "knowledge"—however fallible and arbitrary—deriving from faith. When we then act we use the tools and the weapons which our science and technology provide, and the power with which these instruments now endow us make the precursors of action—including our unspoken and disparaged faiths—of urgent importance.

Karl Popper is a lover of truth and a student of knowing. Accepting great losses, he maneuvers tenaciously, brilliantly, to salvage something of the once-bright vision. Like Kant he believes that "What can I know?" is one of the most important questions a man can ask, and like Kant, also, he is deeply impressed by the knowing which science has achieved. Unlike Kant, however, he lives in an age in which Newton's laws—certainly the best established truths of all time, and presumed immutable—had to be revised. Since then it has not been possible to claim for any law of nature the status of absolute truth.

Popper is a ruthless surgeon, cuts away the gangrenous tissue of epistemology. Verifications, he admits, prove nothing: whenever a Marxist opens a newspaper he finds verification of Marx's theory of history; whenever a psychoanalyst reads a case history he finds confirmation of Oedipal theory. Induction, therefore, is a myth; and no number of confirming instances, however large, can establish truth. Our best established laws, therefore, are conjectures, very well founded perhaps but never, so far as we can know, finally true.

This sounds like surrender. But wait, all is not lost. Though the scientist can never know for sure that his findings are true, "he may sometimes establish with reasonable certainty that a theory is false." If we can't verify, perhaps we can falsify. Now here is a Machiavelli of knowing! Let us turn our backs on truth and proceed directly to storm the citadel of falsehood, then make a separation between that which we have proven to be false and that the falseness of which has not yet been demonstrated. Whereupon, *mirabile dictu*, we shall find ourselves again in the presence of truth, having entered her chambers by the back door. Let us not claim to hold truth in our arms, but be content to stand close by, to feel her charms. Though we may no longer be drunk on her kisses, we still may be exalted by her perfume.

Being human, we must necessarily conjecture about the world; insofar as we also are scientists we shall shape these conjectures in such a way as to expose them to the risk of being falsified by experiments designed to that end. The scientist will ask himself, as it were, "If this conjecture which I now believe to be true were in fact false, what are those circumstances which would most likely expose that falsity?" He will try then to achieve those circumstances, and will regard a conjecture as provisionally true only when it has survived the maximum achievable risk of such falsification, mindful that circumstances more threatening to the hypothesis may later be devised which it may then fail to survive. Scientific theories, therefore, though not verifiable, "are serious attempts to discover the truth." [7]

In his elaboration of these themes Popper has achieved a thorough and convincing analysis of the logic of scientific discovery. But he goes further. Having salvaged so much he reaches also for truth itself—not to claim it for science, but to affirm its existence. There must be such a thing as truth, he argues, since our theories strive to achieve it. That is to say, there is something out there, something real, toward which our theories reach; any one of these theories, therefore, *might* be true; might, that is, achieve perfect agreement with reality; and in that event, though we could never know it, would no longer be conjecture but absolute truth.

So here it is again, that wonderful thing. Truth, which we thought lost forever, comes back as a ghost—out of sight, untouchable, yet in some ghostly way guiding our efforts, and the dignity and value of life shall lie in our trying to get closer to this presence we can no longer grasp. We get the drift of this, but the effort seems desperate as well as noble, and we are not convinced.

There is something out there, and it is indeed real, but not immutable. Our theories do reach for it, striving for perfect correspondence, but the closer we get the more we change it; and when a winged theory manages somehow to wrap its arms around the desired object, the object is altered; not much perhaps, but a little, and in that amount agreement has fled the embrace.

The use of tools is inseparably connected with the development of man, and the master craftsman engaged in his work provides one of the luminous moments of the human spirit. Of Henry Maudslay, inventor of the screw-cutting lathe, one of his fellow workmen said: "It was a pleasure to see him handle a tool of any kind, but he was *quite splendid* with an eighteen-inch file." [8] Machines are but complicated tools, are the direct continuation of that development which began with the stone axe. The steam engine is no more alien to the human spirit than the pulley, and one may still occasionally see—even in these waning times—a mechanic fix a motor in the manner of Maudslay with a file.

Before the machine was slavery. Heroditus describes the building of the pyramids:

Cheops . . . closed the temples and forbade the Egyptians to offer sacrifice, compelling them instead to labor, one and all, in his service. Some were required to drag blocks of stone down to the Nile from the quarries in the Arabian range of hills; others received the blocks after they had been conveyed in boats across the river and drew them to the range of hills called the Libyan. A hundred thousand men labored constantly, and were relieved every three months by a fresh lot. It took ten years' oppression of the people to make the causeway for the conveyance of the stones, a work not much inferior, in my judgment, to the pryamid itself. This causeway is five furlongs in length, ten fathoms wide, and in height, at the highest part, eight fathoms. It is built of polished stone, and is covered with carvings of animals. . . . The pyramid itself was twenty years in building. It is square, eight hundred feet each way, and in height the same, built entirely of polished stone, fitted together with the utmost care. The stones of which it is composed are none of them less than thirty feet in length.[9]

All ancient civilizations included two categories of people, free and slave. In the *Politics* Aristotle describes the relation of master to slave:

The manager of a household must have his tools, and of tools some are lifeless and others living . . . a slave is a

live article of property. Every assistant is as it were a
tool that serves for several tools; for if every tool could
perform its own work when ordered . . . if thus shuttles
wove and quills played harps of themselves, master
craftsmen would have no need of assistants and masters
no need of slaves. . . . The usefulness of slaves diverges
little from that of animals; bodily service for the necessities of life is forthcoming from both, from slaves and do-
mestic animals alike.[10]

Lucius Apuleius describes a flour mill and bakery
about A.D. 165.

Oh, good Lord, what a sort of poor slaves were there;
some had their skin black and blue, some had their
backs striped with lashes, some were covered with rug-
ged sacks, some had their members only hidden; some
wore such ragged clouts that you might perceive all
their naked bodies, some were marked and burned in
the heads with hot irons, some had their hair half
clipped, some had locks on their legs, some very ugly
and evil favored, that they could scarce see, their eyes
and faces were so black and dim with smoke, and some
had their faces all mealy. . . .[11]

In that golden age of Greece of which we are so
proud slavery was accepted by even the most enlightened as a necessary part of the human condition. Pericles speaks nobly of freedom, democracy,
equal justice; but when he says "we" he means free
Athenians; the slaves do not merit even parentheti-
cal exception from his self-congratulatory pro-
nouncements. The exaltation of freedom in the

American Declaration of Independence is written in the same privileged spirit.

When man learned to use oxen rather than men to draw a plow, surely that was a step forward—and another when the tractor replaced the animals. The elimination of slavery parallels the development of machines and the utilization of inanimate energy. Our modern tyrants are no better than Cheops, and they too build pyramids; but the lifting of stone is done by giant cranes, and the energy is fossil oil, not human muscle. Mankind has good reason to view the machine with respect. What is alien to the spirit of man is not the machine itself, but the vision of mechanism, the dreamlike insistence that the universe and all that it inherit, including man, is nothing but a machine, and is thereby knowable as an object, as a machine can be known.

Man stands in a field of dwindling corn, for years has tilled it, sown it, reaped it, and every year the yield has diminished. Why? What would make it grow again? The place is Crete ten thousand years ago and the man knows the answer: the gods are displeased, must be propitiated; he consults a shaman. The place is Kansas, same problem, the man is we, and we, too, know the answer; we, too, consult an expert who tells us what fertilizer to use and how much.

Both formulations purport to be knowledge. In felt conviction they are equal. If we disengage ourselves from the slant of our times is there any objective basis for selecting one over the other? We believe so. With utmost confidence we assert that our knowledge is truer, and that this choice of our knowledge over the Cretan's is independent of place, time, mores, that people of any culture would opt as we, provided they had all the facts. We are sure of this because our formulation leads to predictable results while the other does not. Use the Cretan's knowledge and nothing happens; use our knowledge and the corn grows lush. That is to say, our formulation is truer because it adds to our control. And for no other reason. If the Cretan's formulation led to greater control we would believe it and discard our own.

By this criterion we do know the world better than our forebears. We speak of conquest of nature, control of natural forces, exploitation of resources, victory over disease, mastery of this and that. Our words suggest endless warfare with the world, and we the winner of every battle. And it's pretty much true. We do, indeed, harvest more corn, move more mountains, travel further and faster, wield more power than any men who have ever lived. Our knowledge of the world derived from scientific process is, by this standard, truer than that arrived at in any other way.

Our cognitive vision, therefore, is inseparable from our hunger for power. We would wish it otherwise, would wish our motive were only to know the world. Knowing may be the aim of the individual scientist, but if we as a people consider our drive throughout the Modern Age we find no such disinterest. We want control. "Quest for knowledge" is the banner we follow and we give it to the scientist to carry—and we costume him as idealist and truth-seeker—but hard on his heels, with no banner, come the rest of us who know that knowledge is power, that the fruit of scientific endeavor is useful to our designs on the world and on other men.

"On August 8, 1609," writes Koestler,

[Galileo] invited the Venetian Senate to examine his spy-glass from the tower of St. Marco, with spectacular success; three days later he made a present of it to the Senate, accompanied by a letter in which he explained that the instrument, which magnified objects nine times, would prove of utmost importance in war. It made it possible to see "sails and shipping that were so far off that it was two hours before they were seen with the naked eye, steering full-sail into the harbor," thus being invaluable against invasion by sea. . . . The grateful Senate of Venice promptly doubled Galileo's salary to a thousand scudi per year, and made his professorship at Padua (which belonged to the Republic of Venice) a lifelong one.[12]

Man's control over nature depends upon the state of the agricultural and industrial arts, his power over other men upon weaponry. Technological advance follows upon invention, and invention upon science. The increasingly rapid technological change mirrors a primary acceleration in the scientific processes of knowing. This acceleration has the effect of making the relation between knowledge and power ever more direct and immediate. Decades elapsed after Faraday's discovery of the galvanic current before batteries achieved military and industrial importance. In our century the discovery of radar and transistors was exploited immediately. Now the relation between knowing and controlling has become so clear that every large industrial corporation has a research department. After Hiroshima national states, never inattentive to sources of power, became prime backers of scientific research. It has now become difficult for anyone who wants to know the world to remain unaware that the knowing he achieves will serve that hunger for power and control which has throughout the Modern Age been the driving force behind the quest to understand.

"The modern era," writes Guardini,

was fond of justifying technology and rested its defense upon the argument that techonology promoted the well-being of man. In doing so it masked the destructive effects of a ruthless system. I do not believe that the age will come to rest with such an argument. The man engaged today in the labor of "technics" knows full well that technology moves forward in final analysis neither for profit nor for the well-being of the race. He knows in the most radical sense of the term that power is its motive—a lordship of all; that man seizes hold of the naked elements of both nature and human nature. His action bespeaks immense possibilities not only for "creation" but also for destruction, especially for the destruction of humanity itself. Man as a human being is far less rooted and fixed within his own essence than is commonly accepted. And the terrible dangers grow day by day.[13]

Having accepted that no truth can be altogether objective, should we not cease to concern ourselves with objectivity? What matter more or less? Is not subjectivity in knowing like pregnancy in a convent, whereof the smallest amount is much too much? Let us consider such a swing as this.

Lysenko's fantastic mixture of biology and Marxism could not survive public debate with Vavilov, a scientist who had contributed brilliantly to the development of modern genetics, who sought truth without regard for how it might fit with state doctrine. Lysenko, being a friend of Stalin, found a way, however, to establish the supremacy of *his* truth. On August 6, 1940, Vavilov and several colleagues were on an expedition to the wheat fields of the western Ukraine. In three overcrowded cars they drove from Chernovitsy to the foothills to study and collect plants. "One of the cars," writes Medvedev,

could not negotiate the difficult road and turned back. On the way the occupants met a light car containing men in civilian clothes: "Where did Vavilov's car go?" asked one of them, "We need him urgently." "The road further on is not good, return with us to Chernovitsy. Vavilov should be back by 6 or 7 P.M., and that would be the fastest way to find him." "No, we must find him right away, a telegram came from Moscow; he is being recalled immediately." In the evening the other members of the expedition returned without Vavilov. He was taken so fast his things were left in one of the cars. But late at night three men in civilian clothes came to fetch them. One of the members of the expedition started sorting out the bags piled up in the corner of the room, looking for Vavilov's. When it was located it was found to contain a big sheaf of spelt, a half-wild local type of wheat. . . . It was later discovered to be a new species. Thus, on his last day of service to his country . . . Vavilov made his last . . . discovery.[14]

He was tried, sentenced to death, died in prison of starvation. Efforts to locate his grave have failed. The book in which the Russian geneticist Medvedev recounts these events was denied publication; when it was nevertheless published in America, Medvedev was suddenly committed to an insane asylum.

"We should like to have good rulers," writes Karl Popper,

but historical experience shows us that we are not likely to get them. This is why it is of such importance to design institutions which will prevent even bad rulers from causing too much damage. . . . There are only two kinds of governmental institutions, those which provide for a change of the government without bloodshed, and those which do not. Marxists have been taught to think in terms not of institutions but of classes. Classes, however, never rule, any more than nations. The rulers are always certain persons. And, whatever class they may once have belonged to, once they are rulers they belong to the ruling class.[15]

To seek a truth which will be more objective than some other truth which addresses itself to the same issue does not entail the belief that truth may on occasion be completely objective. One may recognize in all truth an ineradicable subjectivity, yet strive passionately to eradicate as much of it as possible.

Truth heavy with subjective content does not travel well. "Human sacrifice leads to better crops": take that truth to a different culture and you will hang from a cross. A more recent version, "Prayer leads to better crops," fares no better. But "Nitrates produce better crops" may be demonstrated by the response of plants without reference to the identity or preoccupations of the demonstrator, will be accepted equally by Chinese, Arabs, Hindus, and Catholics. Lysenko's truth survived for twenty years in Russia only by imprisoning those scientists who challenged it. A ruling ideal of Western society, writes Popper, has been "our respect for the authority of . . . an impersonal . . . objective truth which it is our task to find, and which is not in our power to change, or to interpret to our liking." [16] The value of this ideal is not diminished but increased by the recognition of its remoteness.

Endeavors of science are accompanied by articles of faith, usually implicit and unexamined. *It is better to know than not to know.* This is a tenet, not a theory, and no more lends itself to scientific treatment than does the Trinity. It comes with our mothers' milk, the air we breathe, is so universal a pre-conception of the Modern Age that we have lost awareness, no longer "know" it. But is it not ob-viously true? Perhaps. But it is not so flatly and fi-nally true that any questioning of it is idiocy. Let us play the fool. Let us remember that the Trinity was once so well established.

Early one morning a man is dressing, stands be-fore the open door of his closet, selects a tie, notes from the top shelf the dull gleam of metal. His sev-en-year-old son plays on the floor. Is it better to know or not to know? "This is a pistol," the man says; "don't ever touch it."

First variation: Two weeks later, the man is out of town on business. Mother wakes at 3 A.M. to a strange noise, opens the front door on a chain, is threatened by a man with a knife. She stands there in a panic, paralyzed, the knife waving at her throat, the man struggling to break the chain. Her son ap-pears at the top of the stairs holding the pistol awk-wardly in both hands; the burglar leaves. *It was bet-ter to know.*

Second variation: For a while memory of the pistol lingers in the boy's mind, then fades. *Knowing made no difference.*

Third variation: The boy and his friend play Sean Connery and Dr. No. The pistol is added to the game. After the explosion fragments of brain drip down the wall. *Better not to have known.*

John Dewey would have knowledge depend on consequences rather than on antecedents, would have all our beliefs shaped by observed effects rather than by conformity to first principles. This distinction separates science from faith, he would say; and our urgent task is to extend the methods of science, its tentativeness and its experimentalism, into all areas of life, most particularly into the realm of social action.

But this itself is faith, How could we ever know for sure that experiment is better than awe, that knowledge is better than ignorance? By noting, Dewey would say, what tends to happen as a result of each. Perhaps. But how far need consequences be observed in order to justify sureness? The scientific revolution is four hundred years old. Is that long enough?

The exploits and conquests of science dazzle us. We cure illness, move mountains, flash pictures round the world, fly to the moon. We control enormous power, but with each gain in power we gain an unexpected segment of impotence. With each gain in knowledge we gain also in ignorance, and live now with new and desperate unknowns. For example, we may or may not detonate so many hydrogen bombs, kill so many people, and so pollute air and oceans with radioactivity that life on earth will end. Such an event, were it to occur, would depend on many things, but one of them, certainly would be our very expert and penetrating *knowledge* of the atom. Were there then anyone left in the midst of that universal desolation to reflect upon what had happened, would he still be an adherent of knowing, or would he conclude that mankind in the twentieth century was like a child playing with a pistol, and that, all things considered, it would have been better not to know?

Or would he perhaps say that not all knowing is cognitive, that we do the word a disservice to link it so tightly with reductive method, and that he who views the world with wonder and with love comes to know it better than he who views it with analysis and logic?

At the beginning of the Modern Age nature replaced divine will, "became the norm," Guardini writes,

which guided man in action and in reason toward whatever was right or healthful or perfect. . . . From this attitude grew a new ethic; the man who was morally good was the "natural" man; so too was the "natural" society or form of government or manner of education or way of life. . . . Nature in short signified and determined a something final beyond which it was impossible to venture. Everything derived from the concept of Nature was understood to be an absolute; whatever could be made to conform with Nature was justified by its very conformity. . . . Nature contained within itself the mystery of the primitive origin and end of all things.[17]

"She is benevolent," wrote Goethe, "and I praise her and all her works. She is wise and silent. No man tears an explanation from her body nor bribes from her secrets that she does not freely give."[18]

This relation of man to nature has come to an end. And so quickly! Only a generation ago Thomas Wolfe could speak still in the voice of Faust: "The dead tongue withers and the dead heart rots, blind mouths crawl tunnels through the buried flesh, but the earth will endure forever. . . ." [19] Man, that is to say, could not change the earth faster than natural processes could restore it, and the great cycle of "seed-time, bloom, and the mellow-dropping harvest" would remain the fixed background against which the chronicle of man is recorded, within which he would find his norms and meanings. It is no longer true. We tear explanations ruthlessly from the body of nature; bribes are not necessary. The mountain we see today will be removed tomorrow for a freeway. Beer cans and gin bottles bob up and down in mid-Atlantic, and we can now so poison the air that the subtle envelope of this planet may never again be the breath of life. Man today, writes Guardini, "experiences nature neither as a standard of value nor as a living shelter for his spirit . . . views the cosmos as a mere 'space' into which objects can be thrown with complete indifference." [20] Nature no longer sustains us, is no longer the rock, the referent of value. We do not now rest in nature's hands, but she in ours. Nature is at our mercy, and, knowing how capricious and impulsive we are, we have good reason to fear for nature's life.

Absolute truth is an obelisk, relative truth is shifting sand. Once we had a vision: from the desert of our uncertainty rose great stone towers upon which, with new materials, we would rebuild the ruined city of St. Augustine. It was a mirage; our eyes sting as we wander through the gloom trying to find it again.

"[Since] no man's authority can establish truth by decree," writes Karl Popper, "we should submit to truth; . . . *truth is above human authority.*" [21] This is a proud motto and a noble purpose: bow to no man but kneel to truth. And we would join this company. But their truth is pure, unmarked by human measure and human meddle, while the only truth we find bears traces of our endeavor. Such truth ceases to be holy, becomes instrumental. The makers of such truth are no longer priests, but lieutenants. We are not sure the knowledge they create defends freedom, but we see how it serves the technocracy, arms the sovereign state. Absolute truth stands alone, instrumental truth is for sale.

The Christian story is full of answers: origin of the earth, creation of man, revolution of the sun, whatever one might want to know; and the Middle Ages accepted these answers as true. With the Modern Age science began an assault on this authority, has progressively dealt with such problems, providing increasingly reliable answers, and bit by bit the Church has given ground. The retreat has not been easy or graceful, but stubborn, often stupid, often mean. In every case science has won, with the effect that the Church now, finally, has abandoned its claim to know the nature of the material universe. No priest now, and no Pope, presumes to inform the faithful about mesons or DNA or the Horsehead nebula.

This long struggle created the impression that science and faith contend for the same domain, that, therefore, as the Church surrenders its dogmas, the realm of faith is diminished while the realm of science is enlarged. By this logic a time will come, unless indeed it is already here, when faith will have been altogether replaced by science. Insofar as this view obtains, we tend to leave decisions, of ends as well as means, to the experts who, we presume, will make them scientifically.

And just here we make a disastrous mistake. For these experts are in the dark as much as we. The giant computers and gleaming laboratories are of no use whatever in telling us the proper ends of human endeavor. Science and faith do not now contend for the same domain, and faith is undiminished by the growth of science. Science has disencumbered man's religious disposition of mistaken myths about the material universe without lessening the degree to which life proceeds on something dark and deep and, however clothed in the garb of reason, ultimately arbitrary. All our ends are lodged in faith, science helps with means. All the great and fundamental questions are answered, if at all, only by leap of heart, by deepest feeling, by faith. What is important in life? What is worth struggling for, and how much? Should I love my neighbor, concern myself with his suffering? How far does neighborhood extend? To the coast? To North Vietnam? Shall I accept violence and murder as necessary to man's life and arm myself accordingly, or shall I declare them elective and work for their elimination? Shall I listen to those who say I can do both? The computers are silent, the test tubes do not react to these queries, and he who concerns himself with them might do better in church than in a laboratory, and the church might better be a forest glade, if any such are left, than the temple of a tired sect.

Increasingly scientists are in the service of governments and corporations, their scientific work serving first the partisan interests of these entities, only secondarily and uncertainly the interests of mankind. All the more reason we should not abandon to them —or to anyone—decisions about ends. The President, we are forever being told, has access to classified information, and this circumstance is invoked in support of the proposition that we should accept his decision to bomb or not to bomb some country. But such a decision involves more than tactics and strategy, more than national security, it involves right and wrong; and since the Reformation it has been our faith, reiterated at Nuremberg, that morality is not to be "classified," that every man has access to it, that no man can delegate it. However great the authority who orders us on a course we believe wrong, it is our duty to disobey.

Science enables us to do more quickly, more thoroughly, and much more extensively whatever faith tells us is right, but nothing in the progress of science justifies diminished concern with faith. We live by it now, as always, for better or for worse. Across every page in history the armies surge, moved by faith to murder, to the ravage of cities, taking with them and using the weapons their technology provides. Looking back on them, it seems to us that much of what they did was madness, crime, and folly. Will our faiths be more generous, more loving, more wise? Too bad for us—too bad for everyone—if they are not; for on our campaigns we too take the weapons our science and technology provide, thereby being empowered a millionfold above the greatest power of even the recent past to do our faith's bidding.

Our scientific endeavor must be controlled by social ends. "But that's what they do in Russia," it is objected; "that's what they did to Galileo; that violates the very freedom democracy is supposed to guarantee." Let us examine this argument, let us re-enter the church of Santa Maria sopra Minerva where Galileo is on his knees before ten cardinals. The Inquisition does represent regnant social value and here, certainly, is controlling scientific endeavor. We do not hesitate, we say to the court, "Leave this man alone. Let him investigate whatever he chooses, let him publish his results, and let him teach. You need not approve and need not assist, but must not proscribe." This view defends the rights of the individual against society; it has been hard-won and we would not compromise it: no scientist shall be barred from any investigation, however foolish, nor from making public his findings. We in the West are pretty much agreed on this. Galileo's problem still occurs in Russia—Lysenko's opponents were thrown in jail, Medvedev was committed to an asylum—but this does not occur in free countries. The modern Galileo in Washington is on his knees, to be sure, and before a tribunal, but is not being disciplined; he is asking for money, and not just a little, but millions. The issue is not whether society will restrict the freedom of an individual, but how society will commit social resources. The lone investigator is free to go his individual way, but most scientific research has become a social endeavor and so must serve social ends.

The danger is that the splendor and mystery of scientific achievement—ever more rapid, and far beyond our comprehension—may so enthrall and intimidate us that we become incapable of acts of faith. For if we cannot, out of faith, generate wise and compelling social ends to be served by science, science will continue nevertheless to produce gleaming means for which ends will later be found by those who hold power—such ends as could be our undoing.

As truth is lost, intentions become more important. When we could believe in a truth that was objective, that owed nothing to us, we could ascribe to it a value transcending our purposes, could believe its goodness to be intrinsic and our pursuit of it pure. Now, knowing that the truth we achieve is changed by the chase and by the achiever, we know no pursuit can be pure. It behooves us more urgently, therefore, to consider what we are about, what we may do with the truth we achieve. For if it should come about that what we do is utterly to destroy the world, then from the far side of that desolation we would cry out—were anyone left to weep or to reflect—that primitive man who viewed the world with awe and wonder *knew* it better than we who fathomed the furthermost secrets of the atom.

Certainty is the basis for attacking evil. Knowing absolutely what is right authorizes the assault on what is wrong.

But certainty is hard to find. Our need is deep, but we see conflicting signs, hear various claims, explanations, revelations, are confused, know not what or whom to believe. When there then appears among us someone who has achieved certainty we gather before him in multitudes. Christ, Mohammed, Napoleon, Lenin, Hitler—they feed our hunger, resolve our doubt; through them we find that which eluded our own vision. In our time we gather before something we cannot see, something too vast and complex to comprehend—probably a computer; we wait, and are told by a technician what we must do. It becomes our certainty, becomes at times that electrifying resolution of doubt for which we always yearn, which all peoples need, which all ages past have found. This certainty then spurs the attack, gives us courage, lifts our heart, sets a plume in our hat, starts banners waving, bands playing. We wear a uniform, inside and out, and on the cobblestones of history booted feet come down in unison. Certainty not only authorizes the attack, often it requires it, creates an aura of gallantry for the murder we are about.

Listen to the seductive voice: "Knowledge is power; there is evil in the world; we must use the power which issues from knowledge to combat evil." The words come from men of good will, and we have always been persuaded. In 1939 Einstein writes Roosevelt advocating atomic bomb research. Science arms us now with such a proliferation of weapons, so much faster than we can use them, each with such an upward-leaping potency, that we are in a position to attack evil more devastatingly than ever before. Is it not conceivable we might eliminate it altogether? In 1948 Bertrand Russell urges that the United States threaten Russia with immediate war. We know, of course, what evil is. The only trouble is we know it differently. For us the evil is communist takeover and tyranny, the end of freedom; for the Russians the evil is American imperialism, all the more dangerous because it is so insistently denied. To act as if we knew for sure when our knowing is unsure becomes more appalling as we who act become stronger.

These reflections do not discredit scientific

method; they discredit certainty, and point out that in our time it is more likely to be achieved by the communion of science and technology than by communion of man with God. Young people in increasing numbers turn away from science—and from reason itself, which has been usurped by science. They look for something holy with which to oppose the oppressive certainties and coercive mandates of a society dominated by the machine. At the beginning of the Modern Age science did, indeed, promise certainty. It does so no longer. Where we now retain the conviction of certainty we do so on our own presumption, while the advancing edge of science warns that absolute truth is a fiction, is a longing of heart, and not to be had by man; that the increasing power deriving from technology is evidence of our increasingly effective instrumental use of scientific method, but not of closer approximation of truth. Our designations of evil are as fallible now as they were ten thousand years ago; we simply are better armed now to act on our fallible vision.

Certainty leads us to attack evil; being less sure we would but resist it. The difference between attack and resistance is the difference between violence and argument, the thread on which our lives dangle.

So briefly do we raise our heads, so quick sink back. For a moment we are lifted by a wave of time, are tossed up into the sunlight of consciousness, may look back then on those others who had their moment, gave a signal. We cannot see so far as where this wave began, it's lost to us, but may watch it coming some thousands of years, rising up, sweeping toward us, can see the faces, hear the voices—that "Farewell!" of Osiander still faintly sounding, a very ghost of voice. Now it's on us, up and up we are lifted, tossed . . . are at the very knife edge. The future is darkness, but the crest of consciousness now using us will use also those who follow, will rush on beyond. This is our moment, the wave is breaking, the crest which passes through us now in tumult was shaped by the past, and we in this moment shape the crest to come—though we will never know what voices linger, what ends we served.

We have lived a delusion, we cannot know the world. Aided or unaided we stumble through an endless night, locked in a range of experience the limits of which are given by what we are and where we live. Earthworm or dolphin, reaching our level of investigative competence, would find a different universe; and we ourselves, in the spiral galaxy of Andromeda, would write different laws. Our eyes have seen the glory, but only within a narrow range, while by us, through us, flow visions for other eyes, music we shall never hear. We are a flicker of joy and grief and need, and shall not see the shores of this dark ocean. May we see but well enough to lay aside the weapons with which we are about to destroy, along with that little we do see, a potential of experience we know not of.

Notes

Numbers in parentheses refer to Works Cited.

EPIGRAPH

Quoted by Popper (24), p. 26. I owe much to Karl Popper whose work I believe of greatest importance. It is an indebtedness and an influence I am eager to acknowledge, the more so as it could not be inferred from my conclusions.

I

THE VISION OF THE MODERN AGE

1. Quoted by Mumford (22), p. 48.
2. Harlow S. Shapley, "Man and his Young World," *The Nation* (May 7, 1924). Quoted by Barnes (1), vol. III: 1105.
3. Bury (9), p. 115.
4. Quoted by Koestler (20), p. 200.
5. *Ibid.*, pp. 202–203.
6. *Ibid.*, p. 203.
7. *Ibid.*, p. 343.

8. Burtt (8), p. 52.
9. Popper (24), p. 5.
10. From the Introduction to (9).
11. Huizinga (16) p. 40.
12. From the Introduction to (9).
13. Quoted by Bury (9), p. 13.
14. *Ibid.*, p. 29.
15. Quoted by Butterfield (10), p. 116.
16. Huizinga (16), p. 31.
17. *An Essay on the First Principles of Government; and on the Nature of Political, Civil, and Religious Liberty.* Quoted by Becker (3), p. 145.
18. Whitehead (30), p. 50.
19 Hume (17), p. 160.
20. Koestler (20), p. 323.
21. Quoted in part by Popper (24), and in full by Koestler (20), pp. 565–66.
22. Popper (24); and Koestler (20), p. 447.
23. Quoted by Bronowski (7), p. 125.
24. Quoted by Koestler (20), pp. 435–36.
25. *Ibid.*, pp. 151–52.
26. Mumford (22), p. 88.

II

THE DREAM OF MECHANISM

1. Woolfe (31), p. 3.
2. Becker (3), p. 7.
3. Hume (18).
4. Koestler (20), p. 340.
5. Quoted by Mumford (22), p. 104.
6. *Ibid.*, p. 104.
7. Quoted in Burtt (8), p. 204.
8. Hume (17).
9. Quoted in Hook (15), p. 148.
10. Quoted by Bronowski (7), p. 255.
11. *Spirit of the Laws.* Quoted by Bronowski (7), p. 271.
12. Guardini (13), pp. 50–51.
13. *Ibid.*, p. 44.

14. Waismann, "The Decline and Fall of Causality," chapter V of (4).
15. T. E. Hulme, *Speculations* (1924). Quoted by Waismann (4), p. 96.
16. Preface to the first edition of *Principia*. Quoted by Waismann (4), p. 95.
17. *Opticks*. Quoted by Waismann (4), p. 92.
18. Bridgman (5), p. 72.
19. Quoted by Bronowski (7), pp. 197–198.
20. R. H. Bixler, *The Saturday Review* (July 2, 1966). Quoted by Pappworth (23), p. 187.

IV

PURSUIT OF THE DIMINISHING OBJECT

1. Quoted by Popper (25), p. 9.
2. In the Introduction to (14).
3. Quoted by Popper (25), p. 42.
4. Percy W. Bridgman, "The New Vision of Science," *Harper's Magazine* (March, 1929), pp. 49–50. Quoted by Barnes (1), p. 1107.
5. Quoted by Waismann (4), pp. 146–47.
6. Barzun (2), p. 323.
7. Whitehead (30), p. 50.
8. Barzun (2), p. 10.
9. Percy W. Bridgman, "Determinism and Modern Science," part II, chapter I in (15), pp. 45–46.
10. Russell (28), p. 561.
11. Becker (3), p. 19.
12. Barzun (2), p. 325.
13. Burtt (8), p. 309.
14. Whitehead (30), pp. 76–79.
15. Guardini (13), p. 48.
16. Barzun (2), p. 338.
17. cf. Bridgman (5), p. 115.
18. *Ibid.*, p. 88.

V
RELATIVITY OF KNOWLEDGE

1. Dewey (12), p. 304.
2. Descartes (11), pp. 29–32.
3. *Meditations.* Quoted in (27), p. 319.
4. Quoted by Russell (28), p. 564.
5. Bronowski (6), p. 90.
6. Huxley (19).
7. Popper (24), pp. 114–15.
8. Mumford (22), p. 115.
9. Quoted by Ubbelohde (29), p. 36.
10. Quoted, *ibid.*, p. 82.
11. *Ibid.*
12. Koestler (20), p. 364.
13. Guardini (13), p. 74.
14. Medvedev (21), pp. 69, 70.
15. Popper (24), pp. 344–45.
16. *Ibid.*, p. 375.
17. Guardini (13), p. 53.
18. Quoted by Guardini (13), p. 55.
19. Epigraph to (32).
20. Guardini (13), pp. 73–74.
21. Popper (24), p. 29.

Works Cited

1. BARNES, HARRY ELMER. *An Intellectual and Cultural History of the Western World*. Three volumes. New York: Dover Publications, Inc. First published by the Cordon Co., Inc., 1937.
2. BARZUN, JACQUES. *Darwin, Marx, Wagner; Critique of a Heritage*. Garden City, N.Y.: Doubleday & Co., Inc., Anchor Books Edition, 1958. Published originally by Little, Brown & Co., 1941.
3. BECKER, CARL L. *The Heavenly City of the Eighteenth-Century Philosophers*. New Haven: Yale University Press, 1932.
4. BLIN-STOYLE, R. J., D. TER HAAR, K. MENDELSSOHN, G. TEMPLE, E. WAISMANN, D. H. WILKINSON. *Turning Points in Physics*. With an Introduction by A. C. Crombie. A series of lectures given at Oxford University in Trinity Term, 1958. New York: Harper & Brothers (Harper Torchbooks: The Science Library), 1961.
5. BRIDGMAN, PERCY W. *The Way Things Are*. Cambridge, Mass.: Harvard University Press, 1959. Copyright © 1929 by Minneapolis Star and Tribune Co., Inc. Reprinted from the March 1929 issue of Harper's Magazine by permission of the author.
6. BRONOWSKI, J. *Science and Human Values*. New York: Julian Messner, Inc., 1956.

7. ———, and BRUCE MAZLISH. *The Western Intellectual Tradition (From Leonardo to Hegel).* London: Hutchinson & Co., 1960.

8. BURTT, E. A. *The Metaphysical Foundations of Modern Science.* Garden City, N.Y.: Doubleday and Co., Inc., 1954. First published by the Humanities Press, Inc., in 1952.

9. BURY, J. B. *The Idea of Progress. An Inquiry into Its Origin and Growth.* With an Introduction by Charles A. Beard. New York: Dover Publications, Inc., 1955.

10. BUTTERFIELD, HERBERT. *The Origins of Modern Science 1300–1800.* Revised Edition. New York: The Free Press, 1965.

11. DESCARTES, RENÉ. *Discourse on Method and Other Writings.* Translated with an Introduction by F. E. Sutcliffe. Harmondsworth (Great Britain): Penguin Books, Ltd., 1968. Translation copyright F. W. Sutcliffe, 1968.

12. DEWEY, JOHN. *The Quest for Certainty.* New York: Minton Balch & Co., 1929.

13. GUARDINI, ROMANO. *The End of the Modern World.* Chicago: Henry Regnery Co., 1968. (Copyright 1956 Sheed & Ward, Inc., New York.)

14. HEISENBERG, WERNER. *Physics and Philosophy, The Revolution in Modern Science.* With an Introduction by F. S. C. Northrop. New York: Harper & Row (Harper Torchbooks: The Science Library), 1962.

15. HOOK, SIDNEY, ed. *Determinism and Freedom in the Age of Modern Science.* New York: New York University Press, 1958.

16. HUIZINGA, J. *The Waning of the Middle Ages. A Study of the Forms of Life, Thought and Art in France and the Netherlands in the XIVth and XVth Centuries.* Garden City, N.Y.: Doubleday & Co., Inc., Anchor Books Edition, 1954.

17. HUME, DAVID. *Dialogues Concerning Natural Religion.* Edited, with an introduction, by Norman Kemp Smith. (The Library of Liberal Arts.) Indianapolis: The Bobbs-Merrill Co., Inc., 1947.

18. ———. "On Miracles." *Essays.*

19. HUXLEY, THOMAS. "The Method of Scientific Investigation." In *The World's Great Literature,* edited by Percy Hazen

Houston and John Kester Bonnell. Garden City, N.Y.: Doubleday, Doran & Co. Inc., 1919.

20. KOESTLER, ARTHUR. *The Sleepwalkers.* With an Introduction
by Herbert Butterfield. New York: Grosset & Dunlap, Universal Library Edition, 1963. Reprinted by permission of The
Macmillan Company (©1959) and A. D. Peters & Company.

21. MEDVEDEV, ZHORES A. *The Rise and Fall of T. D. Lysenko.*
New York: Columbia University Press, 1969.

22. MUMFORD, LEWIS. "The Megamachine—II," *The Myth of the
Machine: The Pentagon of Power* (New York: Harcourt Brace
Jovanovich, 1970). Originally published in *The New Yorker*
(October 17, 1970), pp. 48–141. Second part of four-part arti-
cle.

23. PAPPWORTH, M. H. *Human Guinea Pigs (Experimentation on
Man).* Boston: Beacon Press, 1967.

24. POPPER, KARL R. *Conjectures and Refutations.* New York:
Basic Books, Publishers, 1963, 1965. Reprinted by permission
of Basic Books and Routledge and Kegan Paul.

25. ——. "Quantum Mechanics without 'The Observer.' " Chapter
I of *Quantum Theory and Reality,* edited by Mario Bunge.
N.Y.: Springer-Verlag, 1967.

26. ROSZAK, THEODORE. *The Making of a Counter Culture.* Garden City, N.Y.: Doubleday & Co., Inc., 1969.

27. RUNES, DAGOBERT D. *Treasury of Philosophy.* New York:
Philosophical Library, 1955.

28. RUSSELL, BERTRAND. *A History of Western Philosophy.* New
York: Simon and Schuster, 1945.

29. UBBELOHDE, A. R. *Man and Energy.* Harmondsworth (Great
Britain): Penguin Books, Ltd., 1963.

30. WHITEHEAD, ALFRED NORTH. *Science and the Modern World.*
(Lowell Lectures, 1925.) New York: The Free Press, 1967. Reprinted by permission of The Free Press and Cambridge University Press.

31. WOLFE, THOMAS. *Look Homeward, Angel.* New York: Charles
Scribner's Sons, 1929.

32. ——. *Of Time and the River.* New York: Charles Scribner's
Sons, 1935.

Index